Introducing C A L

A practical guide to writing
Computer-Assisted Learning programs

*TO
JUNE, STEVE,
SUE AND MAX*

Introducing C A L

A practical guide to writing
Computer-Assisted Learning programs

KEITH HUDSON
Writer
formerly Manager of MICRO-T
(Microcomputer training and consultancy)

LONDON   NEW YORK

Chapman and Hall

First published 1984 by
Chapman and Hall Ltd
11 New Fetter Lane, London EC4P 4EE
Published in the USA by Chapman and Hall
733 Third Avenue, New York NY 10017

© 1984 Keith Hudson

ISBN 0 412 26230 4 (hardback)
ISBN 0 412 26240 1 (paperback)

*Printed in Great Britain by
Richard Clay (The Chaucer Press) Ltd,
Bungay, Suffolk*

British Library Cataloguing in Publication Data

Hudson, Keith
  Introducing CAL.
  1. Computer-assisted instruction
  2. Electronic digital computers – Programming
  I. Title
  371.3'9445   LB1028.5

  ISBN 0-412-26230-4
  ISBN 0-412-26240-1

Library of Congress Cataloging in Publication Data

Hudson, Keith, 1935–
  Introducing CAL.

  Bibliography: p.
  Includes index.
  1. Computer-assisted instruction — Programming.   I. Title.
  II. Title: Introducing C.A.L.
  LB1028.65.H83   1984   371.3'9445   84-14264
  ISBN 0-412-26230-4
  ISBN 0-412-26240-1 (pbk.)

Contents

Preface

It is often the case – perhaps more often than not – that new ideas arrive long before there is the means to clothe and deliver them. We can think of Leonardo da Vinci's drawings of helicopters and submarines among many other examples.

Computer-Assisted Learning (CAL) is an example of an idea which has had a particularly long gestation. As I will illustrate early in the book, the principles of CAL were really first discovered by Socrates. As a formal method of teaching, the Socratic method disappeared for over two millennia until the 1950s. It was then revived in the form of Programmed Learning (PL) which resulted from the researches of B. F. Skinner at Harvard University.

Even then, PL was premature. In the 1950s and 60s, methods were devised, such as teaching machines and various sorts of PL text books, and there was a mushrooming of PL publishing at that time. For a complex of reasons – economic, logistical and technical – PL also largely disappeared from the mid-60s, although it continued in a few specialized areas of teaching and industrial training. However, during the same period, PL quietly transformed itself into CAL. But the computerized form was not capable of mass dissemination until recently because personal microcomputers did not have sufficient internal memory sizes. That situation has now changed very dramatically and 128K microcomputers are becoming cheap and widely available. Cheap memory chips of 256K and 1024K cannot be far away, either.

A considerable quantity of so-called educational software is now being written. Some CAL programs have been brilliant and inventive, but many have been of indifferent quality because they have been but bowdlerized, computerized versions of text-book material or lecture notes. Few CAL program writers appear to have paid much attention to the important features of the human learning process now being clearly identified by scientific research in several fields.

CAL, therefore, still suffers from vagueness of definition. As yet, there is still no unambiguous name for the fundamental method of teaching as exemplified by Socrates and developed by Skinner. The most accurate description which also precisely defines the sort of CAL discussed in this book is: self-paced, constructed-response, immediate-feedback, learning program. I have avoided the temptation to foist yet another acronym on the world but no doubt, as the whole gamut of educational software grows and clarifies, a simple name will emerge in due course.

The early iron ships were not made by traditional shipwrights but by bridge-builders. The microcomputer did not emerge from the large computer companies but from small enterprises selling products to do-it-yourself electronics enthusiasts. In the same way, it is entirely possible that teachers and other people involved in traditional training methods will not predominate in the educational software industry that is now growing apace. The field is so new, and the prospects are so enormous, that many writers of intelligence, discipline and creativity will be attracted to this exciting and satisfying activity from many other walks of life.

My original interest in CAL – in its PL form – began in the late 1950s when I read the original papers of American behavioural psychologists. I did not return to the subject until recent years, by which time my initial fascination with PL had been augmented by my studies in brain physiology and the human learning process. I have been influenced by findings from other disciplines, of course, but my principal acknowledgements are to Professor B. F. Skinner and Professor D. H. Hubel, from behavioural psychology and neurobiology respectively, both of whom have been helpful in correspondence.

I must also acknowledge my thanks to my publisher Richard Stileman, and also Claire Gooding, who were keen on the book in its first draft and midwifed it during its later stages. Finally, my thanks also to Irene Jenkins, my hard-working and versatile research assistant and to Jane Ross at Chapman and Hall.

If the book has merit I share it with those above; if the book has faults I incline my head alone.

Keith Hudson
Monkton Combe
Avon

1

Introduction

1.1 CHARACTERISTICS AND PROSPECTS OF CAL

The writing of CAL programs is one of the new information professions and now stands at the door of a large and fascinating future. It is also one of the most creative of the new skills that will evolve in the next few years. CAL writing is not only a deeply personal and satisfying activity, it is also closely linked to two of the most spectacular of all technologies that mankind has ever been involved in – microcomputing and telecommunications.

CAL can be described very simply. It is about the breaking down of information and skills into small pieces. It gives the opportunity to the student to work at the learning task in simple, achievable stages. CAL is not a short-cut to learning nor is it about avoiding the necessary work that is always involved in learning. Also, CAL is not a gimmicky way of dressing up learning in fancy ways.

A good analogy of CAL is that of a car approaching a steep hill. If the car is in too high a gear, it will stall. Long before he reaches it the driver will change down. But precisely the same amount of hard work has to be done by the engine in getting to the top of the hill. This is exactly what CAL is all about. The CAL writer does the gear-changing in the subject – that is, analysing the subject into smaller steps – but the student still has to do the work on those steps.

Active work in small steps, and plenty of timely feedback from the CAL writer (delivered by the microcomputer): those are the essential characteristics of good CAL writing. Having said this, you may infer that CAL writing is, in fact, a highly skilled vocation. The two principal skills that have to be developed are:

(a) The ability to break down large bodies of information into smaller and smaller *quanta* of conceptual steps.
(b) An ability to reconstruct the items in interesting, imaginative and relevant ways by means of well-written and well-presented *frames* on the television or video screen.

The above two skills are what the main body of this book is about – because this is intended to be a *practical* primer on good CAL writing. But CAL actually consists of a whole pyramid of skills and theoretical knowledge. Behind the exterior cladding there are psychological theories, informational sciences, knowledge of brain processes and technological matters which, to a greater or lesser extent, influence the work of the CAL writer. These will be discussed in varying degrees of detail as the needs arise. Some will only be alluded to, and for more information you will have to go elsewhere. A recommended reading list is given for those who wish to read further. In the Tomorrow's world section of the Recommended bibliography, I list some books that can be called parents of this one. These describe, or speculate upon, the broad themes of tomorrow's society – the backdrop against which CAL will develop in the coming years. Three of them deserve special mention: Jonathan Gershuny's *After Industrial Society*, James Martin's *Telematic Society* and Tom Stonier's *The Wealth of Information* [1, 2, 3].

Jonathan Gershuny, an economist, foreshadowed the possibility of home-based CAL before it had taken a few faltering steps. His thesis is that productive machines are becoming so cheap and sophisticated that many services of tomorrow's society will be able to be carried out comfortably within the home. We have already seen the television set taking the place of the mighty cinema chains, washing machines displacing laundries, and do-it-yourself equipment, like electric drills, allowing the home owner to do many of the building and renovation jobs that the previous generation would have called in specialists to do. Gershuny goes even further, to say that many other specialist and professional services will be carried out by the home dweller in the future in the fields of banking, health and education. The only thing that was lacking at the time he prepared his book, besides the microcomputer, was an informational infrastructure. Well, that is now beginning to happen in all the advanced nations of the world in the form of cable or satellite communications.

In *The Wealth of Information*, the title of which is a conscious tribute to the great work of *The Wealth of Nations* by Adam Smith, Tom Stonier is concerned with the pivotal importance of information as an economic resource in the era that is now upon us. As Richard Forsyth said in a review of the book, 'every member of the Cabinet should read it'. Quite apart from its panoramic survey of the history, nature and coming domination of information, the book has some trenchant things to say about the education of those children now being born. Tom Stonier repeated these views in his 1983 Annual Lecture to the British Computer Society, in quite the most radical and forthright lecture the society received in many years, when he predicted:

> a combination of home computers, cheap video machines and an all-important element, good educational software, will enable children to work from home in the near future . . . Schools will still exist as institutions but their role will be

profoundly altered. They will be transformed into places where social and physical skills will be developed rather than intellectual ones.

Thus the economist and the polymath agree. What says James Martin, the computer-guru of the Western world? He has been personally credited with forecasting at least half a dozen of the *major* developments in computing and communications in the last 20 years. Let me quote directly:

> Given a suitable subject and skilful programming, computer (based) teaching can have significant advantages over conventional classroom teaching.

These three books, together with others in the Tomorrow's world section of the Recommended bibliography, are commended to you. The other special section, Brain systems, will possibly appeal to fewer readers, but for those who would like to explore the most fascinating subject of all, the human mind, some of the best books written on the subject to date are listed for your benefit.

CAL programs can be the most boring and impersonal of all teaching methods. They can also be the most vivid, satisfying and productive of all. It is sad to say that many CAL programs at present fall into the former category. But the number of excellent, and effective, CAL programs is growing. The art and science of good CAL writing is improving by leaps and bounds, and the profession is one to which its practitioners can be proud to belong.

Some CAL writers, including myself, are not only proud to be involved, but excited, too. For here at last is a technology that will bring about, for the first time, truly democratic educational opportunities. More than any other educational movement so far, microcomputer-based CAL will be a process that will be largely free of class or culture bias. Moreover – and this is where there is real hope for the planet – CAL technology will become so cheap that the poorest person in the poorest country will be able to participate in it. All this will begin well within the next ten years, and probably within five.

In the remaining parts of this chapter we shall introduce ourselves to CAL by a gentle meander to look at its background and chief features. But from Chapter 2 we shall look at CAL programming in fine detail and will not stop until the final section of the last chapter in which I shall indulge myself in a little speculation about the nature of CAL development in the decade ahead.

1.2 A GENERAL DESCRIPTION

CAL is an acronym, short for Computer-Assisted (or Aided) Learning. There is another similar term, CAI, or Computer Assisted Instruction. Some educational technologists define these terms differently, saying that one is subsumed in the other, and vice versa. The main difference, though, is a colloquial one. CAI tends to be used in the United States (though not on the West Coast) and CAL in the UK.

The beginner will also run into a welter of other related acronyms such as CBL, CBE, CBT, CML, CAMOL, etc. All very confusing. You can regard this as either scholasticism or the inevitable evolutionary struggle within a vigorous new field of endeavour. CBL, CBE and CBT stand for Computer-Based Learning/Education/Training. Of the three, CBT is forging ahead at present. This is mainly to do with the rapid expansion of computer-based training and interactive video within industry. A great number of industries seem to be equipping themselves for substantial in-house training in the years to come.

CML and CAMOL, standing for Computer Managed Learning and Computer Assisted Management of Learning, are somewhat different from those already mentioned. They tend to be used when the computer is being considered as an administrative resource within the educational institution. CML and CAMOL are therefore mainly concerned with timetabling, keeping student records, indexing libraries and so on. Some would like to subsume CAL within CML and keep it under institutional control, but CAL is far too vigorous a youngster for that! He is prepared for the outside world already. CAL will be developed, and will be marketed in ways that will surprise us all.

A tongue-in-cheek definition of CAL is given in Kelly-Bootle's *Devil's DP Dictionary*:

CAL, *n*, (Acronym for CALifornia, or, *archaic*, Computer-Aided Learning). A superior West Coast version of CAI (Computer Assisted Instruction) in which each teacher is replaced with 25 on-line terminals.

We shall use the term CAL in this book. This is concerned with the mutual interaction between the student and the CAL program. The CAL program can be in the form of an audio tape, floppy disc, video disc, video tape, mixtures of them or even downloaded straight into a ROM (Read-Only Memory), or memory chip, from down a telephone wire, cable or from a broadcasting satellite. The machine in front of the student can be the terminal of a mainframe computer or a minicomputer or, as is increasingly likely these days, the stand-alone microcomputer. Let us take a first look at this interaction.

1.3 INTERACTING WITH THE COMPUTER

CAL programs involve the presentation of educational material to the student by means of the television screen or a VDU (visual display unit). The usual way in which the student communicates with the CAL program is by means of the normal (QWERTY) typewriter keyboard. This layout is not the most efficient that could be devised. The most commonly used letters, which ought to be grouped in the centre of the keyboard, used to stick badly in the early typewriters. So these keys are now scattered about. Despite valiant attempts to popularize other, more sensible, keyboards in past years, it seems that we will be lumbered with the present one for ever.

There is another method of entering text into a computer which has appeared in recent years. This is known as the microwriter. This is a small hand-sized device on which a small number of highly sensitive keys are positioned under the fingers of one hand. Letters and other instructions can be obtained by pressing the keys in different combinations rather like playing chords on a piano. Although there are only six keys, the number of possible permutations far exceeds the 26 letters of the alphabet, and a great deal else besides. The microwriter could be the successor to the typewriter keyboard but it is too early to guess at present.

Another way of interacting with the micro has been developed by the manufacturer, Apple, for use with their *Lisa* business system. This takes the form of a small control with one key which, though connected with the microcomputer, can be positioned to suit the user, whether sitting at a desk or more comfortably some distance away. This device is called a *mouse*, a rather silly name, but it has stuck. The mouse enables the user to manipulate the text which appears on the screen. Strictly speaking, it is not a text-entering device so it is unlikely to be widely used in CAL programs though it might have special purposes.

Because the written word is always likely to be important, it is unlikely that the conventional typewriter keyboard, or its equivalent, will ever be displaced from its symbiotic relationship with the microcomputer. Indeed, it is more likely than not that before too long, every schoolchild will have to learn typewriting as a basic modern skill at junior school.

However, there are other techniques which are being rapidly developed for microcomputer–human interaction and these will be widely used both in conventional computing and in CAL. One of these is the graphics tablet. This is a sort of electronic notepad on which the user will be able to draw diagrams, or, if his handwriting is neat enough, write words that the microcomputer will understand. Also, even more interestingly, the microprocessor (the *chip*) is now becoming so powerful that it will not be long before voice-recognition microcomputers will become available. Indeed, some are available now, but are limited to a small number of words and have to be specially programmed to the user's own particular timbre of voice. This will add greatly to the versatility of the home and school microcomputer and to the opportunities it will afford to the CAL writer.

There will also be microcomputers that will talk to the user. These cannot be far off either. However, as far as the CAL writer is concerned, it is more likely that the microcomputer will make use of recorded film on video disc which will both talk and show the face of a human tutor. In this event, the microcomputer, together with the CAL program, will become very *transparent* to the student. That is, the student will feel that he is actually conversing with a human tutor in real-time. In fact, one such system, Apple *Laservision*, has just come onto the market. This is a writer-system but it is far too expensive for the individual CAL writer at present.

1.4 VARIETIES OF CAL

So, we have arrived at a general definition of CAL in that it is a way of presenting educational material to a learner by means of a computer program which also gives the opportunity for individual interaction. We now run into some further difficulties of definition. There is, in fact, a great variety of educational programs which are loosely described as CAL. Among these are drill and test programs, multi-choice tests (with or without accompanying text), educational games, experimental aids, manipulative tests, simulations and a few more which are so idiosyncratic that they cannot be placed in any category. Some commentators include all these within the CAL genre, and they are usually reviewed as such in the educational literature.

The quality of much of this so-called CAL is highly variable. The worst is, without doubt, far worse than the worst possible text book could ever be. One program in O-level English, published by a well-known micro manufacturer, does not know the difference between adjectives and adverbs. This can only create a bad impression. Another program on English literature, published under the imprimatur of yet another well-known manufacturer, described the book, *Eminent Victorians*, as a novel! These lapses are unforgivable.

Undoubtedly, however, the overall quality will improve steeply as more microcomputers find their way into schools. Many of the following sorts of educational programs, not defined as CAL in this book, will, however, find applications within the world of education.

1.5 MULTICHOICE TESTS

Multichoice programs are useful for revision purposes.

1.6 DRILL AND TEST

There is room for these programs in infants' and junior schools for groups of children to have fun together in drills of various sorts. But, generally speaking, drill and test programs, for individual use, are not recommended.

1.7 EDUCATIONAL GAMES

Under this heading we mean programs for the young child which have close similarities to arcade games. It is likely that every child will go through this phase in the same way as he takes up conkers or roller skating at certain ages.

Games programs can be used in two ways. Firstly, they can be used as rewarding interludes in between bouts of more formal learning. Secondly, the whole educational program can be dressed up as a game. Numbers can be added together, for example, by moving railway engines about.

1.8 SIMULATIONS

These can be extremely valuable. They can be short-running animated examples within normal CAL, or they can be written as complete simulation packages. The latter can run in real-time or fast-time. In real-time you can learn how to fly an aeroplane or control an industrial process. In fast-time programs, temporal developments can be condensed into short periods for the learner. For example, you can be a Chancellor of the Exchequer and try to control quarterly balance of payment deficits over a long period of years, or you can become a new entrepreneur and see how you survive in the stressful world of business and banks. Large numbers of variables can be used in simulations, thus taking advantage of the microcomputer's computational powers – something that is not usually needed in most CAL programs. Before too long, as the microcomputer improves by leaps and bounds, simulations which are at present able to be performed only by mainframe computers, such as the Treasury model of the UK economy or the Harvard Business School games, will be available on the home microcomputer.

1.9 EXPERIMENTAL AIDS

The microcomputer can be used as an adjunct to practical scientific experiments, by coupling it to other apparatus.

1.10 IDIOSYNCRATIC PROGRAMS

There will be, it is to be hoped, a constant stream of idiosyncratic programs for the micro. One of these is *Logo*. It was devised by Seymour Papert as part of a broader philosophy about children's education [4]. He is a follower of Jean Piaget in that he believes that the discriminatory powers of young children unfold in discrete stages. Papert and his colleagues at the Artificial Intelligence Laboratory at the Massachusetts Institute of Technology therefore developed a language that would allow the child to discover and refine these newly awakened skills. Part of the use of *Logo* involves a *turtle*, a mobile, recording point or shape on the screen which the child can manipulate. But *Logo* is a great deal more than this and will allow the child to do a great deal of problem solving by means of manipulating text, processing lists of information and recursive programming. *Logo*, or its derivatives, will undoubtedly be a permanent feature of all infants' schools in the coming years. However, *Logo* is not suitable for the highly structured learning that older children need to absorb and thus it will not be mentioned again in this book.

In this book we deal with 'constructed response' CAL. This is a form of teaching program in which the learner has to actively construct a response at every stage. Moreover, the vast majority of these responses will have been anticipated by the CAL writer. In order to achieve this, the CAL writer has to analyse his material, present it in ordered sequences and, subsequently, test that the responses he has called for are, in fact, given. Opportunities are given, however, for incorrect and free range responses and these will be discussed later in appropriate parts of the book.

1.11 CAL MORE PRECISELY

CAL is not a teaching aid; it is a total teaching system. A true CAL program, once loaded into a microcomputer, will take the student from one definable skill level to another without any help or intervention from a teacher or other adult. The microcomputer alone, by virtue of its CAL program, is able to give all the necessary guidance and feedback.

We are now able to describe CAL more precisely to you. It is able to present stimulation to the student in a *structured* way. The microcomputer allows the student to respond *individually, actively, and at his own pace* to the CAL program. Finally, the microcomputer is instructed to give *accurate and immediate feedback* to the student. This is the modern equivalent of Socrates walking in the garden with his philosophy pupils, or of Mark Twain's definition of education as consisting of a teacher at one end of a log and a boy at the other. The technology of CAL, no more and no less, contains *all* the essential elements of a complete teaching system.

A fuller description of the learning process will be given in a later chapter. But for now we must mention one important point. This is that not all learning can be structured. A corollary of this is that CAL is not suitable for some types of learning and for some subjects. To give a very general idea at this stage, CAL is not at all suitable for young children (though *Logo* is, as are educational games). There is at present a vogue in the United States for CAL-type programs for pre-school children. Twenty or 30 minutes a day at *Logo* or some other imaginative program will no doubt be beneficial, but the prospect of some over-keen parents sitting their pre-school children before the educational screen for hours a day is astonishing and deplorable. For one thing, we know far too little yet about the instinctual development of children's learning abilities; for another, so much of children's learning does and should take place within a social environment. Far from turning their children into little geniuses by this means, these parents would do better to give their children as rich a physical environment as possible *and* to ensure that they have sufficient playmates. Our ignorance of the way in which very young children learn is still relatively great. For one of the best informed books on the matter, read Margaret Donaldson's book, *Children's Minds* [5]. It is a brilliant exegesis.

The appropriateness of CAL rises steadily with age as the child completes his basic skills and starts to acquire structured, conceptual abilities. The appropriateness of CAL also depends on the subject matter. You will gain better appreciation of this when we consider task analysis in a later chapter. For the time being we can say that about 40% of the normal range of subjects taught at the beginning of secondary education could be, and probably will be, transferred to CAL in due course. The suitability rises to about 60 to 70% at GCE O-level standard and then becomes even more applicable at higher levels. Indeed, some degree and professional courses could be taught entirely by CAL methods in the future. The prospects for CAL writing are therefore not just confined to children and schools but apply to the whole gamut of skill training for the new professions of the informational age.

1.12 BRANCHING AND LINEAR CAL PROGRAMS

CAL, as it is understood by most writers, has now been described. There are two streams of CAL that must now be mentioned. One is the linear, or extrinsic, CAL program, and the other is the branching, or intrinsic, program.

1.12.1 Linear or extrinsic programs

In this sort of program the student is taken along an almost invariable path from one definable level of skill to a higher one. This path is the most economical one that the CAL writer can devise in conceptual terms. This does not mean that the path always goes as straight as an arrow; it can often deviate and wander about, rather like this first chapter. Neither does it mean that the path is a barren one, containing no examples or analogies. For very good reasons to do with the way in which the brain processes information, a good CAL writer will always seek to enrich his material if it is threadbare. The important point about linear programming is that it doesn't leave loose ends or hint at possible ramifications. It is of constant surprise to the CAL writer that a subject which appears at first sight to be untidy and complicated can, in due course, become extremely orderly. This may take a considerable amount of preliminary study, but the time spent is never wasted.

If a particular subject, such as mathematics, is conceptually complex, then the writer must analyse his material very thoroughly and carefully extract his linear sequences from it. Paradoxical though it may seem at first sight, a conceptually multi-layered subject is particularly suitable for CAL, and even more so for linear CAL. Its very complexity ensures that all its conceptual sinews are properly exposed and delineated beforehand. For someone who is writing a branching program there is always the temptation not to analyse the subject matter thoroughly because he can easily add branches later if the program doesn't test out well. However, this usually doesn't improve matters and the CAL program ends up rather like a dog's dinner – as many business programs are, in fact! That is, it may *seem* to work satisfactorily for most people for most of the time, but you can never be sure that some circumstances might not arise in which the program will *crash*. A good CAL program, like a good commercial program, should be so well structured and documented that later improvements and modifications can be built in without distorting the fundamental aim of the program and its precise objectives.

1.12.2 Branching or intrinsic programs

A branching CAL program is such that, at any important juncture, the CAL writer can allow for different responses by the student. Depending on his answer, the student is then steered by the microcomputer into one of several possible sub-routines before returning to the main path. This has superficial attractions for several reasons, not the least of which is the superb ability of the computer to cope with the highly complicated network of possible pathways that even a fairly short branching program can generate. But the microcomputer should be the servant of the CAL program and not its master; this is not a good reason on its own for using branching.

There are few lengthy branching programs published, for the simple reason that they are almost impossibly difficult to write well. There is another important reason, too, for being wary about writing branching programs. The good student often feels cheated by a branching program because there are so many trails that he hasn't explored. For this reason, an able student will often give a wrong response just to be able to pursue the remedial trail of the writer. There is another reason for wariness, too.

Many CAL programs in the future will be bought in the shops (or *downloaded* from satellite) by private purchasers studying at home. Such purchasers will probably be strongly motivated and are thus unlikely to make many wrong responses. If they have spent good money in buying, say, a long 500K program, they are not going to thank you for filling most of the program with remedial sub-routines. They would sooner pay one-quarter of the price and be taken through the subject in a straightforward way.

Another reason given for the virtues of the branching program is that it enables the better students to make bigger conceptual leaps as they advance through the material. This seems very plausible until you actually try to achieve it. You will find that it is very difficult indeed to allow for students of different 'leaping' abilities. The ever-present danger of writing a program with large conceptual steps is that, although a fast student will certainly *note* important constituents as he speeds through, they will not necessarily be remembered. In fact, there is no evidence that slow, medium or fast learners actually learn in any way differently from one another. The processes that take place in the brain are the same; motivation and speed of response are the only differences.

In this book we shall only be discussing linear CAL programming. However, if you wish later to write branching programs then all the principles described here will be identical and the procedures recommended will be much the same.

1.13 OBJECTIONS TO CAL

The CAL writer will meet with two prejudices. One is against the microcomputer itself and the other is against the CAL methodology. This book does not have to carry the burden of the first charge, but let us discuss the second. The prejudice against CAL seems to be a cultural one deriving from the period of programmed learning (PL) in the 1950s. Very often those who criticize CAL – psychologists and even educationalists – appear to have good credentials. Now the interesting point is this: if you ask them for the precise, scientific reasons for their objections, you are unlikely to hear any.

There are, however, strong attitudinal objections to CAL and, besides the anti-technology theme, they seem to be based on two sticking points. One of them takes the following form: CAL is derived from PL, PL is derived from behavioural psychology, behavioural psychology research often involves learning experiments performed on animals, human beings are not animals, *ergo* the research has no possible relevance to us. The best way to deal with this objection is to meet it head on and ask the critic what is the precise way in which the animal's learning process differs from ours.

Most animal learning experiments use mammals such as rats or cats. Their brains are essentially the same as ours. The only significant way in which our brains differ from theirs is in the amount of what is called polysensory neocortex. That is, we have relatively large areas of neocortex in which abstract thought can be handled, and a rat doesn't (though it has some). But the important brain centres that take part in the learning process, such as the hypothalamus and the hippocampus, are just the same. This is more fully discussed later in the book.

(We are so homo-centric that we *do* tend to disparage the learning abilities of animals. Let me tell you a story. A number of years ago, a neighbour of mine, who'd been troubled with losing some of his chickens' eggs, called me over one evening. At the back of his chicken coop there was a narrow passage hardly wider than an egg. Silently, we watched a rat lying on its back and cradling an egg gently between its feet. Another rat was pulling it along by its tail. The latter was wheezing so I think he was not only a very creative rat, but elderly, too. The moral of this story? Nothing much. It doesn't prove anything – but neither do the emotive arguments of those who criticize programmed learning because it has its origins in experiments on the learning abilities of animals.)

The second prejudice against CAL is that the technology will become part of a sort of centralized society in which we shall all become totally conditioned and controlled. Now this is a much more formidable objection and must be taken seriously. This is a close partner to another important debate about the effects of computers generally – whether they will lead to a more centralized society or whether power will become more decentralized. (This is far from resolved yet. My own view on this point, for what it is worth, is that the microcomputer, together with its access to telecommunications networks, will become so powerful that it will have a decentralizing effect on tomorrow's society. I think this is analogous to the effect of the printed word on government and society in the fifteenth century.) But to return to the slightly different point about the possible behavioural control of society, then we must lay this at the door of the most brilliant of the early researchers in the 1950s, Birrhus F. Skinner of Harvard University.

He opened a new vein of investigating the learning process scientifically. In brief, his learning experiments took the form of controlling the behaviour of animals by rewarding or, more technically, *reinforcing* them. Let us say you want to teach a pigeon how to play table tennis. You allow him to become hungry and then put him into a box containing a small table tennis table and a ball. You roll the ball about until he pecks at it. Immediately you drop a tasty food pellet in. After a little while spent preening and strutting about the pigeon will peck the ball again. You give him another pellet. Gradually, the pigeon begins to peck the ball more frequently. You keep on rewarding him (though not so much that he loses his appetite!) You then start to *shape* his behaviour more specifically. That is, you only reinforce him with pellets when he pecks the ball in a forward direction and disregard pecks in other directions. You then shape his behaviour even more by reinforcing him only for particularly vigorous pecks. This process may only take a few 20 minute sessions. If you train another pigeon to do the same, then you can have them play each other. There is a short film showing this and you may have seen it. In this sort of learning experiment and many others, Skinner and his colleagues measured as many parameters as possible. They also showed that visual skills could be taught. Some animals were even taught to inspect engineering products for cracks on a factory inspection line.

Skinner summarized these learning experiments in a classic paper, 'The science of learning and the art of teaching' [6]. However – and this is where the issue has become clouded ever since – he went on to make some unwarranted conclusions about *all* our motivations and behaviour. Because he had demonstrated that some forms of conditioning (technically, *operant* conditioning) could teach very sophisticated skills, he then went on to say that *all* skills and behaviours could be so conditioned. Skinner rejected the notion that we might have instinctual needs and fairly well-formed instinctual behaviours for the reason that we could never measure them scientifically. Because we could not measure them, they didn't exist. He went on to write a famous Utopian novel called *Walden Two* [7] in which people would live in controlled communities and from which political passions, aggression and crime would be conditioned out of existence. His followers found this book comforting and convincing. Others, however, found it chilling and totalitarian, as I do.

However, it was difficult at the time to put forward scientific reasons against Skinner's claims. Noah Chomsky tried to in an article published in 1959 [8]. He chose to argue with Skinner on just one of his claims: that human language is a totally conditioned acquisition. In a longer work, *Language and Mind*, Chomsky argued that we are born with inherent syntactical structures in our minds [9]. Chomsky had no evidence from brain physiology but argued from an analysis of our grammatical utterances in various human languages. Skinner, unrepentantly and thunderously, replied with *Beyond Freedom and Dignity* [10].

What can we say now, in the 1980s, about the debate? Mainly, people are genuinely worried about Skinner's original thesis about the possibility of a totally controlled society. It would be fair to say that the scientific consensus is that both disputants have been correct up to a point. On the one hand, we are increasingly realizing just how strong early conditioning can be in forming the intellectual and ideological views of individuals. Modern psychologists would agree with the Jesuits' once proud boast: 'Give us a child for seven years and he's ours for life'. Nevertheless, Skinnerian conditioning does not touch upon the more basic human characteristics. These are born anew every generation. During the 1930s and 40s, Stalin, who was a great believer in socio-environmental conditioning, obliterated intellectual and ideological opponents – real or imagined – of his regime in their millions. And yet, even though Russian society has been, and still remains, the most heavily conditioned of any yet known in history, internal dissent, arising from new generations, appears to be as strong as ever.

In any case, as we shall see in Chapter 4, CAL 'conditioning' is totally inappropriate for teaching subjects with high attitudinal content. CAL is really only suitable for subjects which can be clearly analysed into unambiguous Yes/No terms. Subjects like sociology, politics, religion and English literature produce very unsatisfactory CAL programs (though the substratum of facts behind them could be successfully taught, if necessary).

But let us now return to the dispute of the 1950s and 60s between the strict behaviourists and their opponents. This dispute, although highly abstruse and known (or, indeed, understood) by very few people, did affect the overall attitude to behavioural psychology and its physical offshoots, programmed learning texts and teaching machines. The result was that many teachers, liberals and humanistic psychologists formed a powerful lobby against programmed learning (PL). For rather more prosaic reasons (economic, logistical) the use of PL texts and teaching machines began to falter in US schools and it hardly got off the ground at all in this country. If Skinner had modified his original hard-line approach earlier, then the swell against behaviourism would not have grown as powerful as it did. As it was, the overall reaction to strict behaviourism, together with its offshoots, gave the strongest impression to many people that PL itself was somehow scientifically suspect. Nothing was further from the truth. The basic principles of PL remain sound. The main difference today is that we are now much more circumspect as to what skills PL can or cannot be applied to.

In fact, PL continued quietly and productively, mainly within US industry for its own internal training purposes. This was particularly so within the newer high-tech industries like electronics and computing because they had more difficulty than most in finding well-trained people. And then, quietly, companies like International Business Machines (IBM), Control Data Corporation (CDC) and Mitre Corporation started to put PL text into their computers. By showing each frame on a television screen, the learner was able to respond from a typewriter keyboard. Then again, the vast electronic memories of the mainframe computers of the late 1950s and early 60s were able to store the voluminous tests that PL requires (and which bankrupted many a PL book publisher). So, during the 60s, while PL publishers were going to the wall, schools were dropping PL, and behaviourism generally was getting a bad press, programmed learning was quietly forging ahead, particularly within the three large corporations mentioned above.

As PL died, so CAL was born.

1.14 THE 'QUIET' DEVELOPMENT OF CAL FROM THE MID-1950s

The first CAL program, for teaching binary arithmetic, was written by two IBM personnel, Rath and Anderson in 1958. They used an IBM 650 mainframe as their master controller and the students used its console typewriter to interact with it. Soon afterwards, Don Bitzer at the University of Illinois used what was then the most powerful computer in the world, the Illiac I, to present teaching material.

Dr Bitzer's contribution was to decide to use what is now called an *authoring language* or *authoring environment*. This is what amounts to a special computer language which can be made available to CAL writers who are not themselves computer experts or programmers. The CAL writer simply (as was thought at the time!) filled in the frames and the authoring program did the rest of the work in sending the student on to the next appropriate frame.

The philosophy at the time was that the CAL writer's part in the proceedings was a relatively mundane one. It was envisaged that, once CAL was established, hundreds of thousands of teachers, lecturers and industrial trainers could then easily divide their syllabuses into small portions, type them into the computer and then the work was done. The problem, as it was then conceived, was not a matter of program quality but of how to make the method available to as many teachers and schools as possible. There were formidable capital costs involved in buying the master mainframe computers and in laying down expensive transmission lines. Therefore, once enough schools and colleges had enrolled in a local or regional mainframe, the whole educational scene could become industrialized.

It was this viewpoint that lay behind the very large grant of $10 000 000 made in 1972 by the US Government, through the American National Science Foundation (ANSF), to two private companies, Control Data Corporation (CDC) and Mitre Corporation (MC). The hope was that, when the companies were in competition with each other, at least one viable national system would emerge. CDC and MC produced early versions of their systems fairly rapidly. These were PLATO and TICCIT respectively. (For the collector of acronyms these are Programmed Logic for Automatic Teaching Operations, and Timeshared Interactive Computer-Controlled Information Television.) As enjoined by the ANSF, these systems were different in many respects. PLATO used (and still uses) plasma screens which are transparent and allow colour slides to be superimposed upon computer-generated graphics. TICCIT used normal television sets. PLATO distributed its teaching material along ordinary telephone lines to schools (and thence to the individual student terminals). TICCIT used cables. Both forms of distribution have proved to be very expensive. In the early 1970s it was expected that the cost of telephonic transmission would subsequently come down steeply, but it didn't. Cable transmission lines are always expensive because of the physical costs of installation.

Both corporations also adopted distinctly different approaches towards programming. CDC encouraged as many teachers as possible to write material for PLATO using TUTOR, an authoring language that lent itself to a certain amount of flexibility in the way in which a program could be presented. On the other hand, TICCIT adopted a student-orientated heuristic type of format in which the learner can find his own way around the subject matter. This meant, however, that the conceptual analysis of the material had to be done very carefully. For this reason, MC employed their own teams of writers. Each team included an instructional psychologist, a subject matter expert, an instructional design technician, an evaluation technician and a packaging specialist. In fact, the whole approach of TICCIT was of a factory-like production of course material.

The Government subventions to PLATO and TICCIT came to an end in 1977, and from then onwards the systems became self-supporting. What were the results of these massive efforts? Both have been generally considered to have been moderately successful in student achievement results, but not convincingly so. CDC has succeeded in setting up many systems in different parts of the world, including the UK, in which thousands of different programs are available to every student terminal. Indeed, it takes several hours to read through the catalogue of available courses. One decided disadvantage of the PLATO system is the cost of the service. It works out to something like £10000 per terminal a year. This is prohibitively expensive for normal schools and colleges. CDC are developing 'micro-PLATO' versions as rapidly as possible though how these will be marketed in the future is unknown at present. The principal problem of PLATO, it seems to me, is that, although experts are available through the Education Services Division of CDC to help teachers and others, the quality and effectiveness of PLATO CAL programs are extremely variable. Large though CDC is, it is also debatable whether they have the resources to successfully complete the many curricula in which they are involved.

TICCIT CAL programs do appear to have produced improved student performance. On the other hand, students taking TICCIT programs have a higher drop-out rate than on normal educational courses. It would seem that the generally high conceptual ability demanded of TICCIT students doesn't suit all learners. The TICCIT project was, in fact, very much the brainchild of Dr C. Victor Bunderson and it was he who persuaded MC to adopt a unified instructional theory. There has now been a parting of ways: TICCIT being marketed by the Hazeltine Corporation, and Dr Bunderson becoming president of Wicat Inc. The latter company not only produced the first true 16-bit microcomputer but is one of the first manufacturers to devote its principal attention to educational applications rather than commercial applications. However, there has been significant development in the latter area in the last year or two so it is debatable at this stage whether their TICCIT-like CAL system will be prominent in future years.

Before and during the period of the ANSF experiment, IBM, as you might expect, developed their own CAL systems. During the late 1960s they had already built 25 learning centres in the United States. Each of these was controlled by an IBM 1500 mainframe and the students were surrounded by a wealth of technological 'goodies' like light pens, audio players, random-access slide projectors as well as CAL programs. This experiment failed because it was enormously expensive. However, IBM's early teams of researchers went on to spawn many other developments both within and without IBM. Since the days of the IBM 1500 the company has been developing other CAL systems and authoring languages such as Coursewriter-III and IIS. IBM apears to have driven a middle course between the dirigiste policy of MC and the rather more laissez-faire policy of CDC. A sizeable number of good quality programs have resulted, but mainly for the 8 to 12 year old children's market. During 1982 a quite separate division of IBM marketed the IBM PC (Personal Computer). Although this microcomputer is more expensive than others such as Apple, Tandy, Commodore, etc. it has had astonishing success in the home market in the United States. We may therefore expect to see considerable attention being paid by IBM to CAL software for their PC. This will be an interesting space to watch in the coming years.

Another specialist CAL company is Computer Curriculum Corporation, CCC, founded by Patrick Suppes, one of the early IBMers. Dr Suppes developed his system around the PDP-1, one of the outstanding minicomputers of a few years ago. His typical system supports as many as 96 students at once and has been purchased by several school districts in the United States. CCC concentrates heavily on basic school subjects like reading and mathematics.

Even before microcomputers burst upon the scene in the late 1970s there were several more prestigious companies delving quite deeply into the intricacies of authoring languages and CAL programming. Among these can be mentioned Bell and Howell, Texas Instruments and Hewlett-Packard.

The quiet development of CAL may be considered to have ended when 1980 dawned. Already many hundreds, if not thousands, of CAL programs had been written for microcomputers. The whole business of educational computing is now accelerating at a pace that defies the writing of any coherent account. The only forecast I would commit myself to at this stage (1984) is that by the year 2000 the total amount of CAL software will exceed by several times the total amount of industrial and commercial software.

1.15 THE REAPPEARANCE OF PL AS CAL

There are some proponents of CAL who try to disguise its PL origins for fear of arousing the same hostility that affected PL in the late 1950s and early 60s. This is a mistake, because they run into an even greater danger of being criticized by CAL opponents as having no theoretical basis at all. The critics of CAL can charge them with being merely technologically fashionable. By and by, they say, it will all simmer down and we shall be back to the good old fashioned methods. Well, for one thing, the teacher talking to his class is a technology itself – and a very old one. It is the technology of the precious manuscript when there were few to be had. CAL will never beat Mark Twain's gifted teacher sitting on one end of a log and the student at the other, but good CAL is increasingly showing its ability to teach and to motivate in a way that the conventional educational system has never been able to do.

PL is, however, reappearing with a difference, as CAL. In the intervening years since the early learning experiments of Skinner and his colleagues, there has been an explosion of research into the human mind. Disciplines like ethology and anthropology which had been sedate and largely anecdotal before the last war have suddenly revived with great vigour and scientific rigour. These are giving powerful evidence from the sidelines, as it were, about the instinctual behaviours of man. The possibility of these, and even more so, of 'natural' rewards, Skinner could never accept because there was no evidence. Ethologists are showing us that a great number of our behaviours are partially or fully programmed at birth. Our minds are far from being *tabula rasa* at birth. Many of the skills we acquire can never be taught in a structured way. Operant conditioning of a Skinnerian sort can never overcome deep, innate 'programs' in our minds. J. Z. Young's book, *Programs of the Brain*, is well worth reading [11].

Then, too, there has been a brilliant efflorescence of research into the brain in recent years. Some of the best minds of modern science have chosen to study the brain. Among these we can mention Sir J. C. Eccles, Colin Blakemore, David Hubel, Alexsandr Luria, James Olds, Francis Crick, Wilder Penfield and J. Z. Young among many others. Researchers such as these have started to elucidate some of the most sophisticated processes that man has ever studied.

Quite quickly, therefore, in a period of only about ten years or so, knowledge about human nature, about brain processes and learning behaviour has become vastly extended. None of this has overturned the basic paradigms unearthed by the behavioural psychologists of the 1950s. But clearer definitions of appropriate boundaries for PL and CAL have certainly emerged. The learning process, in its different manifestations, is more fully discussed in Chapter 4, and a general theory of learning, interlinking simple facts about the brain and reinforcement theory is given in Chapter 5.

1.16 THE PRESENT RESURGENCE OF CAL

The quiet period of largely 'in-house' development of CAL by IBM, CDC, Mitre and several more commercial companies is now coming to an end. The morning of CAL has gone, and it is now time to say 'Good afternoon'.

The new chaotic phase now starting is, of course, tied up with the fantastic rate of development of the microcomputer. It is not our purpose to give a history of computing in this book, but two salient features will be briefly discussed. One is that the microcomputer is developing at a rate far exceeding its first and second generation forebears, the mainframe and the minicomputer. The other is that the microcomputer has now become a mass consumer product. Over a million personal microcomputers a month are now being sold in the advanced countries of the world and the annual rate is growing at above 50%. Even IBM, which grandly ignored the minicomputer in the 70s, is now busily building personal microcomputer factories all round the world.

One unbelievable fact is now emerging. That is that the personal microcomputer, in about seven years' time, will not only be *just* as powerful as the typical government department or commercial mainframe, but *more* powerful. That seems a crazy statement. How can it be justified? Firstly, let me consider the rate of improvement of the microcomputer. A rough guide to the performance of a computer is given by the formula: $m \times mcf \times bl$. (m, or memory, refers to the amount of information, usually measured in kilobytes, that is internally available to the microprocessor. mcf is machine cycle frequency and refers to the speed with which one package of information can be swept through the machine, or microprocessor. At the present time, mcf is typically 4 MHz, that is, 4 million times per second. bl is short for bit-length, or the size of the package of information that can be transported, or manipulated, simultaneously within the microprocessor, or can be driven out of the machine to a VDU or a printer or down a telephone line.)

Using this performance index the earliest microcomputers of about five or six years ago had a rating of 8. The present–day *average* sort of home or school microcomputer available to the individual purchaser for about £200 to £300 has a performance index of about 1200. If you are clever, and use a microcomputer (or if you are not and use a back of an envelope calculation, like me), you will soon discover that the typical microcomputer is improving every year by a factor of between 12 and 15. In two years the present personal microcomputer will be between 140 and 220 times as powerful. In three years' time the micro you will be able to buy from Woolworth's will be anything between about 1400 and 3400 times more powerful than today's Spectrum, IBM PC, or BBC micro. Another way of putting it is that, at the present time, the typical minicomputer is about 200 to 500 times more powerful than the microcomputer; and the typical mainframe is about 400 to 2000 times more powerful. The personal microcomputer will thus be overtaking the minicomputer in about two to three years' time.

I recently visited a minicomputer department which had a small team of programmers and graphics experts. The head of the department told me that they had designed a complete metallurgical factory for a household–name company, and were about to start on the design of a chocolate egg factory for another! When I mentioned to him that in about three years' time the typical home microcomputer would be able to do this work he was stunned. As he happened to have an old envelope on his desk, it didn't take long to convince him. Of course, minicomputer manufacturers will be able to improve their minis, but not at the rate of 12-fold improvement a year. A better strategy for them is to get onto the faster track of microcomputer production, and this is what they are all doing.

The personal microcomputer will be overtaking the performance of the mainframe computer in about three or four years' time. But the mainframe manufacturer cannot escape so readily onto the faster track, because he has some very important customers who are locked into mainframes, together with their complex software. These customers, like government departments, international banks and the like are controlling systems which are vital in an advanced society. Typically, each such mainframe has needed the additional investment of several hundred programmer-years in the preparation of its vital software. These important customers cannot radically change their computers because they cannot afford the tremendous dislocations that would occur in the preparation of new software, training of staff, etc. They can only do so relatively infrequently. Thus, mainframe production and maintenance will continue for many years yet. However, large companies like IBM and Fujitsu are rapidly diversifying their research and development funds into personal microcomputers on the one hand, and satellite communications on the other. Before too long, 'downloading' software from satellites will be commonplace. This will have big effects on software publishers and the sort of royalties that a CAL writer might expect. This is something that the CAL writer will have to keep a very close eye on.

The above diversion was made just to give a glimpse of the pace of change in the microcomputer world. Before too long, the average middle class home will have a microcomputer *system* as a matter of course, at a price far less than that of the family car. This system will comprise a microcomputer more powerful than the present-day mainframe, a memory that will be able to download a bookful of information in a fraction of a second, the facility to print books and fine-grain colour diagrams, cheap video discs that will be able to hold libraries of information and richly illustrated CAL programs, and a small dish aerial on the roof or stuck in the rose bed in the back garden. The CAL writer is thus going to be involved in an informational revolution of the most radical consequences.

1.17 CAL AND THE JOBS OF TOMORROW

It is now a platitude to say that we are entering the age of information. To some extent, the mainframe in the last couple of decades has accelerated this trend. But it would be more accurate to say that the growth of information has been an intrinsic feature of the industrial society for at least the last 100 years.

A close companion of this information explosion is the vast increase in the number of specialized jobs. The typical job structure of an industrial country before the last war was that of a triangle with a very broad base. This base consisted of a large number of unskilled and semi-skilled jobs. As we pass from these to a smaller number of skilled jobs and then to an even smaller number of professional jobs, the triangle slopes quite steeply to the jobs at the apex, such as Head of the Civil Service or Chairman of ICI.

However, since then the employment structure of an industrial society has been changing steadily into a diamond shape in which there is an expanding number of increasingly specialized white-collar jobs in the middle band. The diamond tapers towards the top, as before; but it also tapers towards the bottom. We have not had this employment structure before, unless we go back about 200 to 300 years when the yeomen of England occupied the broad middle band of occupations and prosperity. The tragedy in recent years is that the rate of change has been so rapid that we have not had the time, even if we knew how, to retrain unemployed people for the new jobs. Even more tragically, many of our school leavers have been woefully unprepared as general office jobs and factory work melted away.

Essentially, the new diamond shaped employment structure ought to be much more satisfactory, and educationally achievable, than the old triangle. After all, in times past, the triangular structure meant, by its very shape, that huge numbers of people in the middle and bottom areas of the triangle were being employed at tasks far below their true abilities. The education system has, in fact, been in the business of frustrating the skill-potential of many people and labelling them as failures in order to approximate the qualification profile of school leavers to that of the employment triangle. But the diamond shape is fundamentally the same as the normal distribution curve of intelligence. There ought to be, and with luck will be, a more natural fit between demand and supply at every ability level in due course.

I am not in any way suggesting that the process of mis-education has been a conscious one or that school teachers should be conspicuously criticized. The education system is part of society and reflects its values and economic needs. In one respect, the education systems of the advanced nations of the world have adjusted to the information explosion. They have become very, very large. And they have also become very, very expensive.

Like the National Health Service in this country, our education system is now vulnerable to 'privatization'. By this I do not mean the expansion of fee-paying schools; they are going to be almost as endangered as the state system. I mean the expansion of more specialized forms of training. Indeed, this has been happening significantly in the last ten years. There has been a steady growth in the number of private companies offering specialized training in the new skills. Some of it seems expensive, but it is also brief, concentrated and effective. I recently asked an honours graduate in computing science how much of his four-year academic course did he think worth while. He replied that his six-months' 'sandwich' course in industry was worth while and about three months of his academic course. Some educationalists would reply that education is more than just imparting vocational skills: it is about life, and a university should give a full, well-rounded experience to young people. This is really a very patronising view of the intelligence of young undergraduates. It would seem that they are considered to be unable to become well-rounded if they enter the world of work and society at, say, 19 years of age. The same specious argument has dominated the whole of our education system since about the 1850s when it was considered undignified for any rich man's son to get involved with merchandising or industry.

Even so, it is likely that the growth in the private sector by normal lecturing and classroom methods will be relatively slow compared with the rate of skills that *could* be taken up by the new industries and services if they were available. We shall therefore not only see the development of CAL for large parts of the normal school and university curricula but also for new specialized jobs. The prospects for CAL are truly quite prodigious. It is noteworthy that every major book publisher in the UK and the United States has started a CAL department in the last 18 months. They, together with several microcomputer manufacturers, are preparing to spend a very great deal of money in developing CAL. They are going to spend even more in a couple of years when broadcasting satellite channels become available and everybody will be able to download good CAL software into their homes.

What can we say, then, as we end this chapter? It is going to be an extraordinarily fascinating future. For those who are prepared to sit down and write good CAL software, then the future is yours. There are going to be many new professions in the informational age, and CAL writing is going to be one of the most interesting and satisfying of them all.

2
Introductory techniques

2.1 THE FRAME

The most obvious feature of CAL is the *frame*. This consists of a short piece of text, or text and diagrams, or perhaps diagrams alone, which appears on the monitor or television screen.

Here is a CAL frame (Frame 2.1). It is the beginning of a dialogue between Socrates and Plato.

Frame 2.1

SOCRATES: If I draw a square like this:

how can I draw another one of exactly twice its area?

PLATO: Please show me.

2.2 THE INTRODUCTION-FRAME

For convenience, the first frame that a student sees in a program is called an introduction-frame, or I-frame. More accurately, an I-frame is one in which a new fact or piece of information is introduced for the first time. In a typical CAL program there will be several I-frames at different stages – usually in the early part of the program – as new material is introduced.

In order for the student to see the next frame we have two alternatives. The first is that, after a reasonable period of time, the micro automatically wipes the I-frame off the screen and presents the next one. This has several disadvantages. For one thing, individuals have different reading and comprehension speeds. What may be a tedious wait for one might be too short for another. Another disadvantage is that, as soon as the I-frame had appeared, the student might have been called away by the front door bell or the telephone. When he returned, the micro would have moved on and the student would have the bother of backtracking (even if he knew how to do so).

Automatic screening, as described, is normally to be strictly avoided. There are only rare occasions when automatically-timed sequences of frames are useful. For example, you may wish to simulate the moving parts of an engine; a sequence of suitably timed frames would give a realistic effect.

On those occasions when you want to move a frame forward when a certain period of time has elapsed, you would incorporate a *time-loop* into the computer program. The latter does not appear on the screen and is in the invisible matrix, usually written in BASIC or machine code.

2.3 CAL WRITERS AND PROGRAMMERS

It is now opportune to differentiate between the CAL writer and the CAL programmer. This book is only concerned with the skills of the former, that is, the person who writes the text of the frames that appear on the VDU. Usually he is also the person who will test the program on volunteer students. When the program is written and tested he may then wish to code the whole program into microcomputer form, but it is not essential. An ordinary programmer can do that. At the present time, a large number of CAL writers are primarily computer enthusiasts and thus write the whole thing. But professional CAL writers normally do not do so.

The relationship of a CAL writer to a programmer in the field of educational software is almost identical to that of the systems analyst to a programmer in commercial software writing. In both cases the former lays down the logical direction and the necessary functions that the program should achieve, and the latter attends to the most economical way in which the computer should be instructed in order to carry the program out.

One of the consequences of the separation of skills is that the CAL writer only has to know the general characteristics of the micro he is writing for. Just as the orchestral conductor does not have to know how to play all the individual instruments in an orchestra, so the CAL writer does not need to know all the detailed specifications of the micro. It is sufficient if he knows the general parameters of the machine such as how much text can be placed on the screen, how many frames he can write, how many diagrams or colours he can use and so on.

However, it will pay the CAL writer to liaise closely with the programmer because a skilled, creative programmer will always want to explore the full technical capabilities of the micro. Consequently, he'll often be able to make suggestions that will vastly improve the layout of the material on the screen or suggest new techniques that the CAL writer could use. This is much to be encouraged *so long as* the CAL writer is the predominant partner and does not lose track of the educational sequence of the program. Many a CAL writer (usually the computer enthusiast) has been carried away by devising pyrotechnical displays on the screen resembling an arcade game and forgets the teaching points he should be making.

From now onwards in the course of this book, I will assume that you are intending to become a CAL writer only. As you will soon discover, there are more than enough skills to be absorbed in becoming a good CAL writer without burdening yourself with the additional hassles of having to code your CAL material once you are satisfied with it. Also bear in mind that, as micros become more powerful, programming is going to become more difficult and time-consuming, particularly as more sophisticated colour graphics become possible. However, if you want to tackle the coding as well, then do so by all means.

But do not rush into coding your CAL program if you decide to do this. As will be emphasized many times in the course of this book, your initial CAL program will need to be tested on some typical students when it is in manuscript form. Invariably, you will have to carry out substantial modifications after such a trial. You will then be wise to test the new version on another group of typical students. Indeed, you may have to enlarge, revise, or modify your CAL program several times before you have an acceptable version. Then, and only then, should you proceed to the coding stage – and from then to the final series of trials on the microcomputer.

Let us now return to Frame 2.1. If you had decided to institute an automatic pause for the duration of the I-frame then all you would need to do is to annotate your manuscript at the side of the frame with '10 seconds', '20 seconds', or whatever, for the guidance of the programmer who will do the coding. He would then write the appropriate time-loop into the computer program to give the pause you required.

2.4 FRIENDLY PROGRAMMING

As already stated, an automatic pause would not be desirable in the case of Frame 2.1. A student might get flustered or lost if the micro continued to plough on whether he was there or not. A program that did this would be called *unfriendly*. We therefore have to consider an alternative method of moving to the next frame, and the student should be instructed what to do next. In this case, the original frame should be amended to look like Frame 2.2.

Frame 2.2

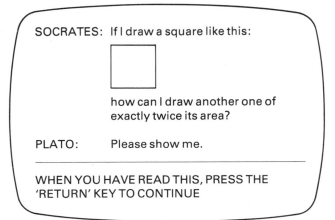

This refers, of course, to the Return key on the micro keyboard. It is advisable that any instruction, such as the above, is clearly demarcated from the teaching portion of the frame, as shown. In Frame 2.2 this has been done by showing the instruction in the upper case lettering and separated from the I-frame proper by a firm line. Once again, annotate the frame in your typescript for the programmer's benefit. Your programmer might suggest the use of a distinct typeface for use with instructions. This is not always possible with existing micros but it soon will be. Well-designed formats on the screen and the use of different typefaces for different purposes are further examples of friendly programming.

2.5 NO-RESPONSE FRAMES

So far, even if your student has read the I-frame and pressed the Return key, you cannot be certain that he has understood it. This is something that the CAL writer has to control. A no-response frame, such as 2.2, has little or no teaching value. There must always be a good reason to write a no-response frame. Many poorly written CAL programs contain long sequences of such frames. This is no better than reading a text book and usually a great deal worse because the student becomes increasingly apprehensive that he is suddenly going to be faced with a batch of questions testing him on all the material that has gone before. And, of course, the student cannot quickly cast his eyes back to refresh his memory as he can when reading a book. So, avoid no-response frames like the plague, unless there is a specific reason for having them.

There are only two good reasons for writing no-response frames. One is when the style or content of a program is about to change radically. (This is not usually desirable but it is sometimes necessary.) One or two no-response frames of a gentle nature – perhaps with some light relief or humour – and which contain no new facts prepare the student for a change of mood or scene. Sometimes it is a good idea to devote a whole frame to generally praise a student for getting thus far into the program. A short sequence of no-response frames is rather like the interlude that occurs between major scene changes in a televison play.

The other reason for a no-response frame is to settle the student in at the beginning of a program. It orientates the student to the style or format of what is to follow. In the case of the I-frame shown above, the student is introduced to an unusual style of presentation, *viz*, a dialogue. The CAL writer is not expecting anything to be learned from this frame, though some students may do so.

The student now presses the Return key and the next frame (Frame 2.3) appears.

Frame 2.3

SOCRATES: If I draw a square like this:

how can I draw another one of exactly twice its area?

PLATO: Please show me.

QUESTION: Socrates has set a problem for Plato to solve. The problem is how to construct a square of . . . . . the size of the first one.

TO MAKE YOUR RESPONSE TYPE THE MISSING WORD

2.6 THE RESPONSE FRAME

There are several important features and points of style in Frame 2.3. First of all, you will notice that it is asking for a response from the student. It is this feature of active responding that clearly differentiates PL and CAL from many other sorts of learning procedures. In short, it is 'learning by doing'. Much research has shown overwhelming evidence that the method of frequent active responses by students is far superior to non-active methods in the speed with which skills are learned or in the accuracy with which facts are retained. The importance of active, continual participation in the learning process by the student cannot be over-emphasized. Even when strict PL or CAL procedures are not employed in the breaking down of tasks into small, regular steps, activity learning is finding its way into all sorts of training, particularly in industry. A great deal of relevant research goes back decades, to before the days of PL development in the 1950s. Yet so much teaching still consists of demonstrations, talks and lectures in front of passive students. The result is that most of this time and activity is largely wasted at best. At worst, it results in boredom and the alienation of the student.

Secondly, notice that the information on the screen is now more complicated and congested. A creative programmer can do a great deal to help the CAL writer to produce a friendly program by the choice of contrasting typefaces, good spacing and the like. Like a good advertisement, a frame should have a sufficient amount of 'white space'. This adds enormously to readability.

Thirdly, you will notice the use of the word 'construct' in the question, instead of repeating Socrates' word 'draw'. The same applies to the change of word from 'area' to 'size'. The purpose of these word changes is to avoid the possibility that the student will respond merely in parrot fashion. If, for example, the question had been:

> Socrates has asked Plato how to draw another square of exactly . . . . . the area of the first one.

then the repetition of almost the identical phraseology could have tempted the lazy student simply to respond with the obvious missing word. In this case nothing much will have been learned even though the response was correct. Mistakes of this sort by the CAL writer are often not revealed until later in the program when it becomes obvious that the fact introduced earlier was not properly learned in the first place.

When a fact is introduced for the first time, it is often difficult for the CAL writer to ask a question or call for a response that is not absurdly easy. Great ingenuity is often required in order to disguise a question so that simple copying is not called for. Wherever possible, so long as the student is not being actively misled, obvious responses should be lightly disguised by word changes, as in the above example, or other methods. However, there will be many occasions when the CAL writer cannot avoid calling for an easy response. But not to worry: the activity of typing in the response will achieve something. In these instances, the CAL writer must ensure that the new fact is called for in subsequent frames in slightly more difficult contexts.

2.7 CUEING THE RESPONSE

Another technical point in Frame 2.3 is the matter of the number of dots the CAL writer should employ to elicit the desired response. In this case, at the beginning of a CAL program, the use of any number of dots other than five dots would actually mislead the student. However, in normal circumstances, it is essential not to cue too heavily by always representing the missing word by exactly the same number of letters. I usually use 10 dots whatever the size of the word or number required as the response. In a friendly program this convention must be clearly explained beforehand. In the case of Frame 2.3 such an instruction would over-congest an already fairly full screen, so this has been left until Frame 2.4.

Frame 2.4

> Socrates has set Plato a
> problem. He drew a square in
> the sand. He then asked Plato
> how he could draw another square
> of .... its area.
>
> ---
>
> WE WILL ALWAYS USE 10 DOTS FOR THE
> MISSING WORD HOWEVER MANY LETTERS IT
> MIGHT HAVE. TYPE THE MISSING WORD.

This frame is testing the understanding of 'twice' that was introduced in the previous frame. Nothing new has been introduced in this frame. Accordingly, Frame 2.4 is called a test-frame or T-frame. It is a friendly frame because, even though a five-letter response is required and 10 dots given, a clear explanation is given below.

It could be that Frame 2.4 is too difficult for the typical student who will be doing this CAL program. This can only be revealed by testing the program on one or more students. If it does turn out to be too difficult then the response can be cued by using 't.........' instead of the above. If this is done then an additional frame needs to follow which tests the response (using slightly different phraseology) by means of an uncued set of dots.

2.8 ENRICHMENT

Also note in Frame 2.4 that some gratuitous information has been given – Socrates drew a square 'in the sand'. The information is of little importance and the CAL writer is not concerned whether the student remembers it or not. But enrichment like this does have some value, particularly for the student with a strongly visual mind. As he reads this frame the student might place the conversation as taking place on the sea shore (although it could equally well be Socrates' garden – and probably was in real life!). Nevertheless, the student might associate this frame and those to come with the picture of Socrates and Plato walking along the beach with the sea breeze gently blowing their togas. So long as a program is not too heavily embellished with such information, then the additional association of ideas that might take place in the student's mind is helpful. If the enriched information does not form an association in the student's mind spontaneously then no harm will be done because the CAL writer will not be calling for this information as a response and the 'writing in the sand' will be totally forgotten.

2.9 TEMPORARY AND PERMANENT MEMORY

The above discussion touches upon a very important feature about human memory that will be discussed in more detail in a later chapter. But, briefly for now, the importance of association of ideas is this. When new facts are initially or tentatively absorbed in the brain they are held in *temporary* storage in a central region called the *hippocampus*. During the first few minutes after introduction the new facts in the hippocampus are in great danger of being forgotten. For example, let us assume that you have been learning a brand new skill. But after ten minutes you received a blow on the head, or fell asleep, or decided to go into the garden and cut the lawn. It would then be highly probable that the new skills you had started to learn would be completely forgotten. Another example that is very common is reading (and under-standing) a bedside novel for several pages and then falling asleep. Taking up the book the next day reveals that you had totally forgotten what you'd read!

In the initial period after the new facts have entered the hippocampus it is vitally important that they start to make connection with pre-existing knowledge held in *permanent* storage in a region of the brain called the *neocortex*. If this occurs then it is much more likely that the new facts are not forgotten. If the new facts are kept alive and recycled in the hippocampus for more than about 20 minutes then they will almost certainly start to make connections with memories in the neocortex, no matter how absurd or illogical they are. What happens is that a sort of pulsing, radar-like process occurs by which the new facts are offered to the neocortex. If any sort of association can be established between pre-existing ideas in the neocortex and new ideas in the hippocampus then a process of permanent memory starts to take place. For a period of several hours the new information is pulled out of the hippocampus and laid down by permanent changes in the nerve networks of the neocortex.

Now if a student is learning a task that is totally new to him, or something which is rather barren of rich associations of ideas (such as the present geometry problem) then any additional help in forming links with the neocortex is useful. It is likely that most of the associations between the neocortex and the hippocampus will be done unconsciously and automatically by the brain, but some additional possibilities, such as Socrates writing in the sand, can only help.

2.10 THE TEST-FRAME

Looking back at Frame 2.4, we have already mentioned that this is a test-frame or T-frame. This follows the I-frame in which 'twice' was introduced. Every I-frame should always be immediately followed by a T-frame, and perhaps several more. The distribution of I-frames and T-frames within a CAL program is of the greatest importance and we shall see later how the CAL writer should document this as he proceeds through a program. Without a concurrent record, the CAL writer can easily start to drift away from the teaching objectives of his program and, in fact, produce something which doesn't teach and is very boring.

2.11 CUEING AGAIN

The student has replied with 'twice' in Frame 2.4. Here is the next frame (Frame 2.5).

First of all, notice that there are 10 dots, even though the desired response, 'square', has 6 letters. The student should not now be puzzled by this. It would be slightly worrying to him, however, if one of the alternative responses, such

Frame 2.5

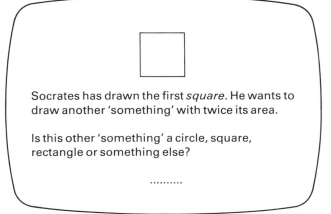

Socrates has drawn the first *square*. He wants to draw another 'something' with twice its area.

Is this other 'something' a circle, square, rectangle or something else?

....

as 'rectangle', also had 10 letters. This is something that the skilled CAL writer will avoid in the early stages of a program.

Nevertheless, the student might be slightly mystified by the novel appearance of 'circle' and 'rectangle'. These will briefly compete in his mind before he settles upon 'square' as the correct response. The correct response has been cued pretty heavily by underlining its appearance in the first paragraph of the frame, even though there is no logical reason in this frame why it is correct. (There may well be a trace memory, but the fact that Socrates wants to produce a square from the previous frames means that the CAL writer cannot assume that the student will have remembered this.)

Although 'square' has been mentioned in a previous frame, it has not been formally introduced and called for as a response. Frame 2.5 is therefore another introduction-frame or I-frame. As you might expect, this I-frame must be followed immediately by a T-frame (Frame 2.6), testing the retention of the new concept learned. Note that care has been taken in Frame 2.6 to avoid *verbal* cueing of the required response, 'square'.

Frame 2.6

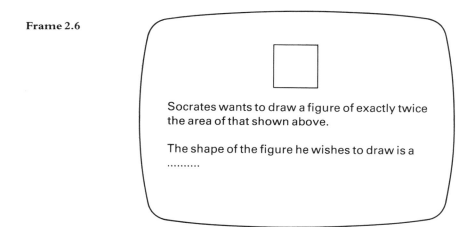

Socrates wants to draw a figure of exactly twice the area of that shown above.

The shape of the figure he wishes to draw is a ....

At this stage, the student is beginning to understand the precise nature of the problem that Socrates is setting. The 'twiceness' and the 'squareness' of the problem objective have both been introduced and both have been tested. However, experience and research shows that salient facts like these are not thoroughly absorbed by a student (even in temporary memory in the hippocampus) until they have been correctly responded to on at least six or seven (or even more) occasions. Therefore, these two facts need to be called for in several more frames before the CAL writer can be sure that the student has thoroughly absorbed the objective that Socrates is after. The next frame (Frame 2.7), therefore, tests both these facts again.

Frame 2.7

Socrates has drawn a shape in the sand. He is
going to show Plato how he can draw another
..........-shaped figure of .... the area of the first
one.

2.12 THE LINK-FRAME

The 'squareness' and the 'twiceness' of Socrates' problem have been tested
again in Frame 2.7. This time both responses have been called for. The two
parts of understanding the problem are now being associated, or linked,
together. For this reason Frame 2.7 is called a link-frame or L-frame. An L-
frame is actually a test frame; but whereas the T-frame is a term used for the
simple testing of a single fact immediately after its introduction, an L-frame is
more complicated and usually links together at least two facts, and often
several more.

There are many more L-frames than other sorts of frames in a CAL
program. They become progressively more difficult as the facts, skills or
concepts become more precise in the student's mind. The purposes of the L-
frames are to associate, compare and contrast the information introduced into
the program in a progressively more discriminating way.

So far, in Socrates' problem, we have called for responses to do with
'squareness' and 'twiceness' three times each: once (each) in an I-frame, once
(each) in a T-frame and once (together) in an L-frame (Fig. 2.1).

Frame number	1	2	3	4	5	6
Type of frame	I	I	T	I	T	L
'Twiceness'		1	2			3
'Squareness'				1	2	3

Fig. 2.1

Frame 2.8

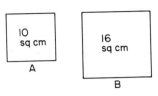

A is the first shape that Socrates drew. Is figure B the answer to his problem? Well, it is certainly ....-shaped, but it is not .... the area of A, so it is not the answer.

Frame 2.9

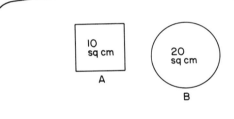

A is the first shape that Socrates drew. Is figure B the answer to his problem? Well it is certainly .... the size of A but it is definitely not a .... Thus B is not the answer to his problem.

Some more L-frames are still desirable (Frames 2.8–2.11).

Although Frames 2.10 and 2.11 are only asking for a single response (a 'Yes' or a 'No') they are both testing both aspects of the problem. They are both L-frames, therefore.

The record of the CAL writer's progress so far is as in Fig. 2.2.

The writer can now be reasonably sure that the two important criteria in understanding Socrates' problem will be understood by the student. He cannot be completely sure, however, until he has tested the sequence with typical students.

Frame 2.10

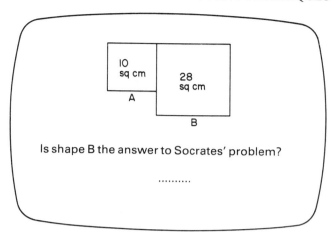

Frame 2.11

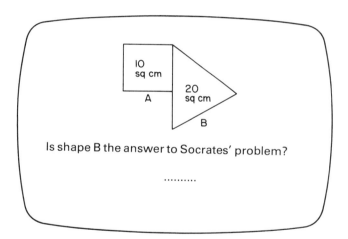

Frame number	1	2	3	4	5	6	7	8	9	10
Type of frame	I	I	T	I	T	L	L	L	L	L
'Twiceness'		1	2			3	4	5	6	7
'Squareness'				1	2	3	4	5	6	7

Fig. 2.2

2.13 PREREQUISITE KNOWLEDGE AND ABILITY OF THE STUDENT

The CAL writer also needs to be reasonably sure about the ability and knowledge of the typical student who is going to start his program. In the case of the program already shown, the writer assumed that the student would already have a good grasp of the concept of area. If this were not so then 'area' would have to be introduced, tested and linked with the other information. In this case the CAL writer's record of the CAL frames might then be something like that shown in Fig. 2.3.

Frame number	1	2	3	4	5	6	7	8	9	10	11	12	13	14	15	16
Type of frame	I	I	T	T	T	I	T	L	L	L	I	T	L	L	L	L
Area		1	2	3	4			5	6	7				8	9	10
'Twiceness'						1	2	3	4	5			6		7	8
'Squareness'											1	2	3	4		5

Fig. 2.3

Note that frames 13 to 16 contain various permutations of the linkages that can be made.

2.14 NATURE OF DISTRIBUTION

Looking at the diagrams so far it may seem that new information in a CAL program should be introduced in a regular fashion – presumably continuing in a clockwork manner until the end of the program. This is not so. For one thing, new information introduced towards the end of the program is likely to be completely forgotten because not enough associations will have been formed during the short time they were temporarily stored in the hippocampus.

Another reason why new facts, concepts or skills are not introduced in a regular manner is that all of them are not of equal novelty or complexity. If, for example, you were learning the names of the bones of the foot, then it would be likely that the names would be of equal novelty and of similar complexity. But in most CAL programs such uniformity rarely occurs so that the regularity of Fig. 2.3 is seldom achieved. So, in considering the information that he is going to introduce in a program, the CAL writer will have to exercise a great deal of skilled judgement in deciding the relative importance that should be given to one new concept or another as they are introduced, tested and linked with others. The only strict rule I observe is that every I-frame is immediately followed by at least one T-frame. How many more T-frames and

L–frames are used for that particular fact depends upon its importance. At the end of the day, the distribution of the frame types will be determined by the outcome of the trials carried out with typical students.

2.15 CONTINUING THE SOCRATES PROBLEM

The Socrates problem has been unusual so far in that I have been using it to illustrate some important principles of CAL program construction. In actuality, Socrates did not have to prepare the way for Plato in the way I have done. The dialogue I have chosen is just one of many that took place between Socrates and his pupil. From previous tutorials, Plato would have been able to grasp the essence of Socrates' problem immediately. So, in real life, Socrates proceeded from the question in Frame 2.1 to an instruction which I have represented in Frame 2.12. The frames that follow (Frames 2.13–2.21) show the way in which Socrates proceeded to solve the problem – or rather, how Plato did under the carefully constructed guidance of his tutor.
(At the present time, light pens are becoming widely available. These enable micro users to draw lines on the screen.)

Thus Plato (with Socrates' help!) solves the problem.

2.16 TRY-IT-YOURSELF

Frame 2.1 and then Frames 2.13–2.21 are faithful CAL translations of one of Socrates' real dialogues with Plato, taken from the latter's book, *Meno*. As Plato recorded it years after the event, he undoubtedly condensed some of the intervening steps and associations that are a normal part of a CAL program.

Frame 2.12

SOCRATES: Well, first of all, draw another square of the same area at the side of mine.

PLATO:

Frame 2.13

SOCRATES: Now draw two more squares of the same size directly underneath.

PLATO:

Frame 2.14

SOCRATES: How much larger is the big square than one of the smaller squares?

PLATO: .... times.

Frame 2.15

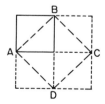

SOCRATES: That's right. The big square is four times larger than the small one. That's too large for what we want. Draw some diagonal lines from A to B, B to C, C to D and D to A.

Frame 2.16

SOCRATES: Do the diagonal lines cut the small
squares exactly in half?

PLATO: ....

Frame 2.17

SOCRATES: Are the diagonal lines of equal
length?

PLATO: ....

Frame 2.18

SOCRATES: Do you agree that the diagonal
lines have, in fact, produced a new
square?

PLATO: ....

Frame 2.19

SOCRATES: How many halves of the small squares does the new diagonal square consist of?

PLATO: ....

Frame 2.20

SOCRATES: How many halves does each small square consist of?

PLATO: ....

Frame 2.21

SOCRATES: So if the new diagonal square is four halves, and the original small square is two halves, how much larger is the diagonal square than the original small square that I drew?

PLATO: ....

However, all the important steps are there and it is a superb example of a programmed sequence of learning despite the fact that it is 2500 years old! Try these frames on your friends and if you get any wrong answers write some additional frames.

2.17 A TRAILER ON REINFORCEMENT

Finally, if you can imagine Socrates talking to Plato, he would have responded to Plato's answers with encouraging smiles, 'yeses', nods and so on. These 'social rewards' are, in fact, an extremely important part of such a dialogue, even though they cannot be easily recorded on paper. The technical term for reward in the context of learning is called *reinforcement*. What is the role of reinforcement in the learning process? How can a micro reward a student? These are some of the questions we shall answer in the next chapter.

3
Reinforcement

3.1 REINFORCEMENT OR REWARD

In Socrates' original tutorial he would have encouraged Plato's progress by all sorts of nods, smiles, murmurs or 'that's right's. This feedback is technically called *reinforcement* or, more usually, reward. In the 1950s, Skinner and his associates would not accept the use of the term 'reward' because that implied that there were natural events that could be called rewards. But we know now, from brain research, that many of the things or events that reinforce learning are, in fact, 'natural' reinforcers. They *do* have a special role in the brain because they have survival-value for the person concerned.

   This definition accords with common sense and it is good to see common sense and scientific research lining up together. If Skinner could not have originally accepted food and water as natural reinforcers he would certainly not have accepted nods or smiles. Yet the evidence is that these social rewards are, in fact, natural reinforcers in the same way. There is a large area of the brain devoted solely to remembering people's faces – very large numbers of them (usually far larger than we can remember names for). There is also evidence that many social skills – and, of course, the rewards and punishments that go with them – are instinctually programmed and reveal themselves in full-blown form, or near it, at definite stages during childhood. There is a very good reason why social reinforcers are needed by the individual. During the hunter–gatherer period of human evolution it was imperative that a mechanism evolved by which individuals were encouraged to remain in the tribe. In the open savannah, individuals or families would not have survived for long. Nods and smiles, therefore, are among the most powerful reinforcers known to man. Another strong reinforcer is 'knowledge of results' and this is discussed in Chapter 5. Accordingly, in his tutorial session with Socrates, Plato would have been receiving a mixture of both social and 'knowledge of results' reinforcement when he correctly answered Socrates' questions.

   We have no problem giving 'knowledge of results' reinforcement on the present-day microcomputer. This can be done by saying 'Yes' or 'No' or simply by repeating the correct response. As far as social reward is concerned we shall, in the not too distant future, have all manner of listening–talking–video micros that will give accurate simulations of personal feedback. Until then, we are confined to giving social reward by means of presenting encouraging words on the screen. Let us look at a 'settling-in' I-frame from an O-level Economics course (Frame 3.1).

Frame 3.1

In an economics examination you will almost certainly be faced with at least one question on International Trade.

These questions are straightforward *if* you can recall about 20 discussion points in a logical order.

Sometimes it is hard to remember them all so we are going to arrange them in a Memory Grid for you. We will keep this Memory Grid for the rest of this Unit. Using it, you will be able to summon up all the important facts instantly.

PRESS RETURN TO CONTINUE

As soon as the Return key is pressed the programmer arranges for Frame 3.2 to appear.

Frame 3.2

The specific points you'll need to remember about International Trade are given by three memory words centred around 'TRADE' as we show below: INTERNATIONAL T R A D E

	R	R	S
	A	O	T
	D	U	U
	E	N	A
	S	D	R
			Y

From the memory grid you'll be able to remember that the three memory words are:
T .... A .... E ....

TYPE YOUR RESPONSES AND PRESS RETURN

This is a genuine I-frame because it is introducing information for the first time. It would seem that the CAL writer is throwing an awful lot of new material at the student, such as 'memory words', 'grids' as well as 'trades', 'around' and 'estuary'. However, this CAL Unit is one of many that make up the whole Economics course and the student will already have become acquainted with some of these terms.

3.2 THE RESPONSE AND IMMEDIATE REINFORCEMENT

The student obeys the instruction and types his responses to Frame 3.2. (The instruction, by the way, is a standard one for all CAL programs in this Economics course, and needs mentioning only once at the beginning of each Unit.) As soon as he has typed the remaining letters of 'TRADES AROUND ESTUARY' the screen automatically changes to Frame 3.3.

Frame 3.3

> The specific points you'll need to remember about International Trade are given by three memory words centred around 'TRADE' as we show below: INTERNATIONAL T R A D E
>
> ```
>                                    R      R       S
>                                    A      O       T
>                                    D      U       U
>                                    E      N       A
>                                    S      D       R
>                                                   Y
> ```
>
> From the memory grid you'll be able to remember that the three memory words are:
>
> TRADES ...   AROUND ...   ESTUARY ...
> **TRADES   AROUND   ESTUARY**

The asterisks are intended to convey the fact that the programmer has arranged for the confirmatory words to flash a few times a second in order to enhance the reinforcement effect. How quickly should the programmer arrange to supply the knowledge of results? *It should be done almost immediately afterwards.* To be more accurate, it should be about 0.6 second after the student has made his response. Technically, this is called *latency*.

This latency of 0.6 second is of the highest importance and crops up repeatedly from quite different research sources. One of the reasons why Mark Twain's teacher sitting at the end of a log is so effective is that he can reinforce the boy within this latency period. Ordinary conversations are examples of mutual reinforcements with superbly-timed latencies. These reinforcements consist of smiles, nods and verbal encouragement given from one talker to the other as soon as each has finished. Ethologists study conversations like these by means of analysing frozen frames of a recorded video film every hundredth of a second or so. An answering smile to a statement also occurs about 0.6 second later and thus has maximum effect on the person who has just spoken. All this is totally unconscious, of course, but the remarkable constancy in the latency suggests an evolutionary origin.

Latency was first discovered by Pavlov from his experiments in the *classical* or *reflex* conditioning of dogs. When a bell had been associated in the mind of the dog, then the sound of the ringing bell alone would initiate salivation about 0.6 second afterwards. Skinner rediscovered this from his *operant* conditioning experiments already mentioned. His subjects learned quickest when reinforcements occurred 0.6 second after their responses.

The effectiveness of the latency of 0.6 second has even cropped up in computer research. At Yorktown Heights, one of IBM's prestigious research centres, a team under Walter Doherty, investigating the performance of computer systems, discovered an unexpected effect of reaction times upon the productivities of people who were designing chips using highly interactive graphics screens [12]. Figure 3.1 shows the amazing upturn in the abilities of the users that occurs when the computer is able to respond between 0.3 and 0.6 second after instruction.

For this reason IBM has set a goal of 0.3 second as the optimum response time for all its internal systems for the future. They consider this latency important enough to be universally applied in the coming years to ordinary business use of their computers for productivity reasons. How much more important is it that computers which are presenting educational programs observe this rule of latency?

Yet several manufacturers of CAL authoring systems are falling down very

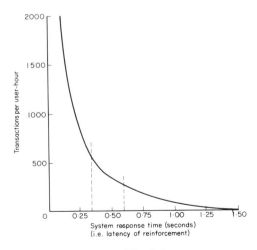

Fig. 3.1

badly in this respect. After a learner has typed in his responses some systems have a latency of several seconds before the reinforcement appears. Why this is occurring is that the programmers are putting the operating system of the CAL program into the microcomputer, but the data remains on disc. That is, once the student has responded, the appropriate reinforcement to appear on the screen has to be hunted for from the disc. And this can cause an appreciable delay.

The importance of a very short latency has to do with the ability of a brain nerve cell, or *neurone*, to respond to the reinforcement. A brain neurone that has just 'learned' something by being activated by the student's response very quickly loses its sensitivity unless a wave of reinforcement follows rapidly. It is the latter that starts to produce permanent change in the neurone. That is, it makes it even more sensitive on a later occasion to respond in the same way when the student is considering the same information. Even a delay of a few seconds causes the learning ability of the neurone to decline steeply.

So what appears to be a triviality turns out to be of the highest importance. Your programmer should be aware of this and ensure that a 'time loop' of 0.6 second is incorporated into the program between the student's response and the reinforcement which appears on the screen.

In fact, this 'triviality' will have some technological consequences. Later on in this book good reasons will be given why the bulk of CAL programs should be long enough to give a student between 40 and 60 minutes of intensive study in one session. Such a program is a long one in present-day microcomputer memory terms. A program of this duration will have to contain at least 30 to 50K of operating instructions and about the same at least for the data and graphics that appear on the screen. If reinforcement is to be instantaneous, or nearly so, then it will have to be interlaced with the rest of the program. This means, in practice, that all the CAL program, of at least 100K in total, must be able to be loaded directly into the microcomputer's internal memory. With even modest colour graphics, a 40 minutes program could easily amount to 200K. The largest ordinary home or school micro at present (early 1984) is of 32K or 48K. But the 256K RAM chip is not far off. One of its suppliers, NEC, is already distributing samples to micro manufacturers and they will be widely available, no doubt, during 1984.

Let us now return to examples from the Economics program to show other variations in reinforcement (Frame 3.4).

In the above case the student might be puzzled as to how to start his response. He can be helped in this by the programmer, who arranges to have a flashing cursor on the first dot, as shown by the asterisk.

About 0.6 second after the student completes the response, the screen changes to Frame 3.5.

Your programmer has produced an attractive graphics word for you. (By this we mean that the typeface shown is not normally resident in the

Frame 3.4

> You'll be able to recall these three memory
> words by imagining a small river barge of the last
> century called a 'lighter'. Its skipper would earn
> his living by unloading (or 'alighting') cargoes
> from ocean-going clippers. So imagine a lighter
> that *trades around* a river *estuary*.
> Complete the memory grid:
>
> INTERNATIONAL T R A D E
>   * . .
>   . . .
>   . . .
>   . . .
>   . . .

Frame 3.5

> You'll be able to recall these three memory
> words by imagining a small river barge of the last
> century called a 'lighter'. Its skipper would earn
> his living by unloading (or 'alighting') cargoes
> from ocean-going clippers. So imagine a lighter
> that *trades around* a river *estuary*.
> Complete the memory grid:
>
> INTERNATIONAL T R A D E
>   R R S
>   A O T
> *Correct!*   D U U
>   E N A
>   S D R
>   . . Y

microcomputer, and the programmer has had to design this typeface specially, by means of a graphics generator.)

Let's move on to the next frame (Frame 3.6).

If the student successfully completes Frame 3.6, then the micro responds with pseudo social reinforcement, 0.6 second later (Frame 3.7).

None of us can have enough praise! Don't be mean. Make full – even lavish – use of the verbal equivalents of social rewards.

In Chapter 2, the Socrates program introduced 'twice' and 'square' separately, being careful to introduce them, test them, and ultimately link them together in order to understand the problem that Socrates set. In this case, however, we have introduced and tested the whole three-word

Frame 3.6

All the important points that you'll need to remember on International Trade can be summoned up by jotting down the three words
....

Frame 3.7

All the important points that you'll need to remember on International Trade can be summoned up by jotting down the three words
TRADES.... AROUND.... ESTUARY....

Well Done!

mnemonic as one unit. The reason for this is that it is vital for the student, when taking the examination, to recall *all* the important facts about international trade. Actually, in this Economics program, the memory word 'Trades' summarizes the *advantages* of trade, the word 'Around' summarizes some of the *disadvantages*, and the word 'Estuary' summarizes the techniques which governments use in order to *restrict* international trade. In the usual O-level examination, a question might ask for comments on at least two of these matters, and often all three. So it was considered important that all three memory words were learned as one entity. If the examination question asked for a short essay on the advantages and the disadvantages of international trade it would be disastrous if the student could only remember one of the memory words. Also, the three word mnemonic was tied to the word 'Trade', as in 'International Trade'. So, in an examination question on the subject, a whole chain of responses should be generated instantly: 'International Trade' produces 'Trade' which produces 'Trades Around Estuary' which then gives 19 particular points for discussion. This is what the rest of the Economics unit is concerned about.

3.3 SCHEDULES OF REINFORCEMENT

We have used two sorts of rewards, or reinforcers, so far. One is a 'knowledge of results' method by repeating the student's correct response. The other is by saying 'correct' or 'yes' or 'well done' as a social reward by the use of praise.

So far, we have implied that reinforcement is given on the successful completion of *every* frame. This is called *continual reinforcement*. It has, however, one major disadvantage, and this was discovered by Skinner in the 1950s. This is that if reinforcement is withheld for one reason or another – perhaps by accident – then the learner's behaviour soon drops away. This can be put the other way round. If a student can be weaned away from needing continual reinforcement (carefully, and in a special way) then his *motivation* to repeat his newly learned skills will be higher, even if he is not rewarded every time. In other words, he will be better motivated to revise what he has learned.

Let us now recap on what we know about memory and add some more by means of a story. Let us imagine that, late one afternoon, a student called Len completed a 40 minutes CAL Unit on the advantages and disadvantages of international trade. He got every response correct and he was reinforced every time. During those 40 minutes, all the relevant facts were well associated and rationally ordered in his short-term memory, his hippocampus. At the end of the 40 minutes session he successfully answered an examination grade question. Also, during the 40 minute period we know that some of the new material in the hippocampus was already beginning to lay down permanent networks in his long term memory, the neocortex.

In the evening, Len went to a football match, drank a couple of cokes with his friends and then came home to bed. He had a good night's sleep and woke up at eight o'clock, after his mother had been calling him for 10 minutes, with a pleasurable memory of a dream he'd just had in which he'd scored 240 goals. Now *we* know – though Len doesn't – that during the course of watching the football match the previous evening and during the night his hippocampus was continuing to feed his newly acquired facts about international trade to his neocortex. After then, it was possible that some especially epic goal he'd seen at the football match was also fed through to permanent storage.

Len has his breakfast. Then we catch him. 'Len', we say, 'how would you like to answer the question on international trade again?' He wouldn't! So we have to bribe him with the promise of a Cup Final ticket if he'll do this for us.

So he sits down and retakes the question he'd successfully answered the previous day. At the end of the test we check his results and find that Len has not remembered all the facts, only about 90% of them. This wouldn't be serious if he were taking his examination that morning, but it's actually three months away! The likelihood is that Len would only remember 50 or 60% at that time *unless* he revised his material in the meantime.

Let's have another look at his breakfast retest. He had 'forgotten' 10% of what he had learned the previous evening, even though he had worked hard on the program and had got it right every time. 'Forgotten' has been put in inverted commas because no new facts or ideas, once in the neocortex, are ever truly forgotten. New information which has been properly associated in the neocortex actually causes permanent chemical and physical changes in the brain nerve endings. These changes do not reverse. What does happen, however, is that the new networks can be modified, interfered with or short-circuited by later information. It is quite possible, in Len's case, that some of the memories of the football match which followed his study session actually did a take-over bid for small parts of the new international trade networks. The international trade network is still there in Len's neocortex, but has become harder to recover. Len spent 40 minutes getting the new facts into his neocortex. If he spent only 5 minutes the next day in revising them, then the complete network would be redefined to its former state. It would probably become even better because it would strengthen itself against any stray football memories that intervened.

Now this is not a deficiency of CAL alone. This loss of definition is something that affects all learning, whether it is acquired by CAL methods or any other. However, if we can help to motivate him to revise his newly acquired facts, then all the better. Motivation can be helped by *intermittent* reinforcement. So, in a CAL program, once the student has acquired the necessary facts or skills, testing should be repeated several times and rewards gradually, though randomly, withheld. Before we discuss this further let us return to our program on international trade for a couple of frames.

Here is Frame 3.8.

Note that the flashing cursor is still used. Note also that the format on the screen has been changed once again, even though the same three word response has been called for. This is to avoid a process called *habituation* by which identical data is 'screened' out of consciousness. Always rearrange your screen formatting when repeating identical or similar material.

The student now types his response. Usually, if he is correct, the micro will send a rewarding message onto the screen. This time, however, *there is no reinforcement at all*. The micro ignores the response and shows the next frame (Frame 3.9).

Frame 3.8

Complete the memory grid:
I N T E R N A T I O N A L

T *.........
R
A ....
D
E ....

Frame 3.9

'TRADES' is our first memory word and its six letters will give you six reasons why it is beneficial for a country to carry out international trade.

Because 'TRADES' has six letters it is going to be able to remind you of .... (advantages/disadvantages) of a country's international trade.

3.4 INTERMITTENT REINFORCEMENT

Behavioural research has shown that intermittent reinforcement maintains a higher motivation in the student to practise the new skills he has learned [6].

The purpose of this section is a practical one. It is to remind you to keep a record of frame-types as you write them. It can now be used to keep an additional record of the pattern of reinforcement for each fact that is involved in the Unit. We show a specimen record below. To keep matters simple let us assume that we have started a CAL Unit in which we want to teach four new concepts, *viz* A, B, C and D. The frame record looks like Fig. 3.2.

Note the following points:

(a) The L-frame in frame 3 is linking the newly-introduced concept A with something learned in a previous program.
(b) Every I-frame is followed by a T-frame.
(c) The regularity of the I-frames shows that the CAL writer considers that A, B, C and D are about equal in difficulty.
(d) The first no-reinforcement frame does not occur until frame 13. It is not until then that the writer is reasonably sure that A and C are well on their way to being safely acquired by the student.

Complicated though such a record seems to be, it is the only way in which the writer can maintain control of the material in the Unit. Without such a frame record the Unit can get hopelessly tangled within a small number of frames. In reality, keeping a frame record takes up hardly any time when frames are being written.

Figure 3.2 doesn't give an adequate picture of the intermittent reinforcement of the program. The next 30 frames (Fig. 3.3) show concept A alone for simplicity.

This is the record of a program that ends at frame 45. Notice that the non-reinforced frames become more frequent towards the end. Final test-frames at the end are not reinforced at all. For another example of a frame record see Chapter 7.

Frame number	1	2	3	4	5	6	7	8	9	10	11	12	13	14	15
Frame type	I	T	L	I	T	L	L	L	I	T	L	L	L	I	T
Reinforcement?	✓	✓	✓	✓	✓	✓	✓	✓	✓	✓	✓	✓	■	✓	✓
Responses?	✓	✓	✓	✓	✓	✓	✓	✓	✓	✓	✓	✓	✓	✓	✓
Concept A	1	2	3			4	5	6				7		8	
Concept B				1	2	3	4	5					6		
Concept C									1	2	3	4	5		
Concept D														1	2

Fig. 3.2

3.5 THE FINAL TEST-FRAME

This is the last type of frame that you need to become acquainted with. Usually, FT-frames are comprehensive sorts of L-frames which contain most, if not all, the facts, skills or concepts that have appeared in the program. The last FT-frames of all are usually not reinforced because they approximate to the educational objectives of the Unit – and these may be actual examination questions, or parts thereof.

Frame number	16	17	18	19	20	21	22	23	24	25	26	27	28	29	30
Frame type	L	L	L	L	L	L	L	L	L	L	L	L	L	L	L
Reinforcement?	✓	✓	✓	■	✓	✓	✓	■	✓	✓	■	✓	✓	✓	■
Responses?	✓	✓	✓	✓	✓	✓	✓	✓	✓	✓	✓	✓	✓	✓	✓
Concept A	9			10		11	12	13			14	15			16

Frame number	31	32	33	34	35	36	37	38	39	40	41	42	43	44	45
Frame type	L	L	L	L	L	L	L	FT	L	L	FT	L	FT	FT	FT
Reinforcement?	✓	■		✓	■	✓	■	✓	■		✓	■	■	■	■
Responses?	✓	✓	✓	✓	✓	✓	✓	✓	✓	✓	✓	✓	✓	✓	✓
Concept A	17		18	19				20			21		22	23	24

Fig. 3.3

3.6 TRIAL AND ERROR LEARNING

In real life we learn as much from our mistakes as from our successes. Accordingly, some CAL authorities, most notably Roger Hartley, of the Computer Based Learning Unit at Leeds University, consider that a CAL program should contain up to 30% frames which allow for *incorrect* responses [13]. This is something that the early behavioural researchers in the 1950s did not allow for. In their early learning experiments with animals, responses that were incorrect were simply not reinforced. In this way, as has been described, quite intricate performances could be 'shaped' by carefully selected reinforcement. This matter of only reinforcing potentially correct responses carried on into the early programmed texts that were written by B. F. Skinner and others. This became a sacred cow of early programmed learning.

However, we now know that 'knowledge of results' (hardly applicable to most animals) constitutes a strong natural reinforcer in its own right. In some cases it hardly matters whether a student replies correctly or incorrectly, so long as the reinforcement from the micro carries the correct information as to whether the student was right or wrong.

3.7 INCORRECT RESPONSES

If we accept that incorrect results are capable of teaching the learner, we must be careful to ensure that the frames concerned contain fair questions. Students should never be induced to respond incorrectly. Frames which are written to allow for incorrect, as well as correct, responses, are called *experiential* frames. That is, they reflect the experience of everyday life and the mistakes we are constantly making. These experiential frames are discussed in more detail in Chapter 7.

Another practical question must also be considered. This is that if we write frames that are capable of a large number of possible mistakes, then the CAL writer cannot possibly anticipate them all and the programmer cannot allow for them in the coding. A program containing many opportunities for trial and error learning would also take longer to complete than a program in which all its frames are to be successfully answered. So some sort of balance must be struck between the program which is totally educational and an experiential one in which there are some elements of trial and error.

This must be left to the CAL writer. It is a good idea to have one or two experiential frames in the first draft of a program and then wait and see what turns up during testing. You may then feel that a suitably placed opportunity for a student to make a mistake may prevent later mistakes that occur from normal frames. Make your experiential frames simple with the opportunity for only one mistake.

4
Principles of structured learning

What is *structured* learning? It is the learning of those skills, concepts, information, habits or whatever which lend themselves to being clearly analysed beforehand. In this way they can be presented economically and efficiently to the student. The same skills, etc. could be learned in an unstructured way – that is, by trial and error – but it would take so much longer.

There are, however, many skills which are so complex that it would be beyond the wit of the most brilliant tutor to analyse and set up a learning structure. These unstructured learning skills are instinctual. A new-born baby already possesses some skills such as sucking, grasping and rudimentary interpretation of the bewildering kaleidoscope of shapes, colours and sounds. All this is a prodigious learning task for his brain, and so overwhelmingly complicated that only automatic brain programs could possibly cope with it. The learning curve in the first few days develops faster than at any other time of his life. Acquiring all these skills takes place without any adult intervention at all, though some of them begin to merge into what can be called semi-structured skills.

Semi-structured skills are also very complex. Unlike the unstructured skills of seeing and hearing, however, semi-structured skills need the participation of adults. The principal adult concerned, of course, is the mother. The mother doesn't teach the child in a systematic and conscious way. Indeed, there is some evidence that her skills of motherhood also start off in an instinctual way and she needs time to perfect them. Just as the unstructured skills of the baby merge into the semi-structured skill, so do the latter merge into another group – structured skills. In these we can just begin to glean the first conscious striving to acquire and manipulate perceptions in the form of concepts.

Let us look in slightly more detail at unstructured and semi-structured learning skills before we proceed to structured learning. It is important to grasp the differences, even if we cannot draw hard and fast demarcation lines between them. This will help us to avoid those pitfalls that affect those who try to apply CAL in inappropriate areas of learning.

4.1 INSTINCTUAL SKILLS AND UNSTRUCTURED LEARNING

Learning how to see or hear are two good examples. A baby learns to see or hear simply by being exposed to a variety of sights and sounds. There is nothing that parents can do to affect this in any significant way. In the early days and weeks of being born a baby will be so overwhelmed with new information to process that he will 'turn off' for most of the time by falling asleep. Falling asleep is not a passive or defensive act; during sleep all the important information that he has gained during brief periods of wakefulness will be laid down permanently in his brain.

This is where we meet one of the characteristics of the human brain (and animal brains, too) that surprises the layman. The brain is not at all eager for information. In fact, it is so constructed that most information is resisted, not allowed to enter. The brain only allows information that is *significant* to pass through into important processing areas. Most of the brain cells, or *neurones*, are what is known as *inhibitory* neurones. Their function is to screen information and prevent most of it getting any further. The other main sort of neurones, *excitatory* ones, are pushing information forward. There are many more inhibitory neurones than excitatory ones. The brain can therefore be imagined as a filtration device which is mainly preventing the mass of information from getting through.

At birth a baby is born with almost all the neurones that he will ever have. Unlike other sorts of cells in the body, neurones do not regenerate; they can only die. They are kept alive by being used. Their purpose is to transmit (or block) short, sharp electrical discharges from one to the other. These electrical messages travel along very thin, hair-like projections that radiate from the centre of the neurone. It is really the number of dendrites that make the difference between a well-functioning brain and a poor one. At birth the neurones are furnished with relatively few dendrites. Most of the dendrites at birth belong to excitatory neurones and are thus pulling the information in from the eyes, ears and other sensory cells in the body with great alacrity. However, all this information would soon overwhelm the brain into an epileptic seizure unless the baby sleeps and new inhibitory dendrites are formed. Therefore, although no new neurones are formed, a forest of new dendrites and connections between neurones begins to grow from the moment of birth.

The baby thus becomes increasingly able to cope with the mass of information coming in. Automatically, at one filtration stage after another, very sophisticated networks of dendrites develop. The phantasmagoria of shapes, sounds, colours, strange feelings from the skin and so on gradually become clearer and sharper. All the filtration stages that we will ever need during our lifetime are *in situ* at birth and will develop if we are exposed to the information they can cope with.

This leads on to another important consideration. And this is where parents can help, though not control, instinctual unstructured learning. Gradually, as the filtration stages develop, the baby needs as rich an environment as possible. As the baby grows older and stays awake for longer periods more filtration stages become available in his brain for development. However, if some sorts of information from the environment are not received by the brain then the dendrites in those filtration stages do not develop. If this deficiency continues for weeks or months then the dendrites do not grow and the relevant neurones die.

A considerable amount of research has been carried out on this effect. The most prominent researcher in the UK is Professor Colin Blakemore and his book, *Mechanics of the Mind*, is strongly recommended [14]. His experiments have been mainly carried out on cats, whose brains are very similar to our own. If a kitten is brought up in an environment in which there are no vertical lines, for example, the particular neurones in the filtration stage that 'sees' vertical lines will die. The adult cat will never be able to see vertical lines. The appropriate neurones cannot be resuscitated.

This feature of unstructured learning undoubtedly applies to us no less than to animals. An early missionary to the Kalahari bushmen in the last century built a small meeting house. But the adult bushmen wouldn't go anywhere near it. This was not because of any cultural objections to the missionary (though they might have had those, too), but because they couldn't 'see' the meeting house clearly. It seemed mystifying and forbidding to them. The reason was that they had never had to interpret vertical lines before. The small number of trees in their area were spindly and ragged; their own huts were made of grass and were round. At birth, the Kalahari bushmen had the potential to see vertical lines. But the particular area of the brain that would have been involved was never activated.

Such sensory deprivation in early childhood can, in fact, lead to bizarre interpretations of what appears to others to be obvious. Charles Darwin came across another interesting example of this when his chip, *HMS Beagle*, laid anchor in a bay in Tierra del Fuego. The natives, in their dug-out canoes, saw the shore party coming ashore in their rowing boat and welcomed them. They thought that the *Beagle*'s crew had rowed from across the ocean. It is reported that they couldn't even 'see' the *Beagle*, with its strange shape and sails, even though it was in full view in the bay!

In this book we are concerned with the presentation of information from *outside* the brain. For this reason we have called instinctual learning *unstructured*. There is no way in which we can help such learning by structuring information. All we can do to help is to shield a new-born baby from being overwhelmed with information by avoiding loud noises and, later, as the baby grows older and is able to cope, by ensuring that enough variety of sights, sounds and experiences are available. Touch is also extremely important.

Paradoxical though it seems, a rich environment allows the full development of all those areas of the brain that can the more successfully inhibit information – that is, to apply fine discriminations between what information they will accept and the vast majority of insignificant information that they will inhibit.

One of the ways in which a good mother will enrich a baby's environment is by talking a lot. This accelerates enormously when the baby makes his first (instinctual) communications by gurgling and smiling. From now on the baby starts to learn semi-structured skills. Although, as Piaget has shown [15], many other automatic and instinctual learning skills develop at different stages for many years to come, the child, even at a few weeks old, reaches the stage when adults are necessary if the child is to acquire some skills. We will now look at this form of learning.

4.2 SOCIAL SKILLS AND SEMI-STRUCTURED LEARNING

If, by now, you are ready to accept the notion that animals learn in much the same sort of way that we do, let us give an excellent example of semi-structured learning by means of the young chaffinch. At a certain stage of adolescence the chaffinch suddenly acquires a full-blown song. This is instinctual. Just as with the child learning to hear or to see, no adults are necessary. A young chaffinch brought up in a soundproof room or reared by blackbirds will still explode into chaffinch song when it is ready. However, the song is a very rudimentary one. If the young chaffinch continues to be reared without hearing adults or being able to sing to other adolescents then the song remains crude. When he is an adult his song will not be recognized by other chaffinches. He will not be able to protect territory or to woo other chaffinches. His song needs to be refined by getting feedback from other chaffinches. Gradually his song becomes perfected. Not only does it become the full-scale, versatile performance of the adult chaffinch, but it also has the characteristic 'dialect' of its locality.

An ornithologist can place an adult chaffinch to within a mile or two of its place of origin. The same can be done, of course, in the case of humans, though in our case there is a social, as well as geographical, dimension. The skill of speaking is acquired so early in life that only the most persistent efforts later in life can obscure the early dialect. The early conditioning in childhood will resist possible effects of standard 'BBC English', no matter how frequently it is heard. Indeed, there is some evidence that, in our densely packed cities, local dialects are intensifying rather than moderating.

Exactly the same process occurs with many human skills, particularly social skills. Let us rejoin the mother of our previous example and her baby who is a few weeks old now. The baby has started to smile from some deep instinctual program. The smile is probably the most powerful social behaviour of all. It is needed for the important reason that a human child is largely helpless for a considerable time. Some strong transactional tie needs to develop between mother and child.

The baby's smile triggers a large amount of new behaviour from the mother. By and large, this new behaviour is teaching behaviour. Although the mother is not consciously following a tutorial pattern, she is now engaged in shaping and teaching the broadest and most important subject of all, without which human civilisation could not exist. By this we mean social skills. This includes smiling, laughing, singing, pacifying, co-operating – and talking.

It is this matter of the ability of humans to talk that occasioned the dispute between Skinner and Chomsky that has already been mentioned in our opening chapter. As a reminder: the former believed that all human verbal behaviour was conditioned. The latter believed that the detail of human grammar and syntax was deeply implanted in the human brain at birth. The modern view is somewhere in between with a slight leaning towards Chomsky rather than Skinner. There is, for example, a part of the human brain a little above the left ear, called Wernicke's area, which is indispensable for producing sensible, logical sentences. Although Wernicke's area probably does not embody human grammar in any detailed way at birth, it has 'filter' systems which must be activated in the very early years of the child.

We are therefore born with a strong potential to talk and this will persist for several years. But if someone doesn't learn to talk in childhood then it can't be done later. The neurones in Wernicke's area will have become atrophied. Some very rare human evidence confirms this. There have been a few documented cases of 'wolf children' when children, abandoned at birth or lost soon afterwards, have been adopted by wild animals. Cases have occurred in which wolves and baboons have been the pseudo-parents. In all cases, when the child has been subsequently found at more than about 10 to 12 years old, he has been unable to learn to speak. The child has been able to learn many other skills, but not to talk. Less rare have been those instances in which Wernicke's area has been totally destroyed by brain damage. If the unfortunate person is a child under about 12 years old, then a rudimentary 'shadow' Wernicke's area over the right ear is able to develop. Within a year or two the child is speaking as well as though no accident had occurred. But a teenager of 15 or 16 or an adult will never be able to speak again. No amount of conditioning can ever revive the skills.

There is thus a strong predisposition towards acquiring many skills like speaking. Adults and others are absolutely necessary for the skills to be fully developed. However, skills like speaking are so complex that nobody is ever likely to know how to formulate ideal learning conditions. To some extent, ethologists are beginning to understand some of the important methods by which mothers teach their children to talk. They do this by filming them and then examining the film frame by frame. Many of the important interchanges that occur between mother and child are impossibly fast to observe normally.

They are largely instinctive and are given and received subconsciously. So although there probably are ideal teaching rules for some learning skills, many of them may always remain unobservable. Even if they are able to be codified in a theoretical way from film analysis, they will be impossibly difficult to practise.

The ability to be truly bilingual – that is, to be able to *think* in two languages – is also something that must be acquired in childhood years. The older one grows the harder it is to learn to speak a second language. Children brought up in a bilingual or trilingual household can acquire other languages as adults without much effort. All those brought up in a strictly one-language home find it difficult to be able to speak another language and are certainly never able to do so without a give-away accent.

What are the skills that fall within the semi-structured family? They appear to be those skills in which there are enormous disparities in adult life. For example, brilliant musicians exist who have skills qualitatively different from anything that most ordinary people can acquire. Prowess in art, dancing, athletics and manual dexterity also seem to be skills which cannot be fully acquired by formal methods later in life. They are impossible to structure unless the skills have got off to a good start very early in life.

The purpose of the discussion so far in this chapter is to emphasize that learning methods cannot always be formulated. Some skills cannot be taught at all and either emerge full-blown at birth or in rudimentary form. Some of these skills merge into others which, while definitely taught by parents and others, cannot be formulated. None of these skills lend themselves to PL, CAL or, indeed, any other formal teaching methods. These can only build upon what has been already started.

There is another characteristic of both unstructured and semi-structured skills. This is that they are all *composite* skills in which high levels of both conceptual *and* physical skills are involved. Even apparently 'passive' unstructured skills like visual interpretation also need movement and manipulation before they can develop to a high level. In understanding what we see we also need to move towards and around objects, to suck them and to manipulate them in early childhood.

Some remarkable experiments have been done along these lines. For example, two kittens were not allowed to see vertical lines from birth, except for brief periods of the day inside a round booth. They were both strapped (gently) into gondolas which hung from a centre pole. One kitten only was allowed to walk by means of holes in its gondola. He therefore walked round and round, taking the other passive kitten around with him. The upshot of all this was that the 'walking' kitten was able to see vertical lines as an adult, while the passive one could not! This example anticipates what is covered more thoroughly in Chapter 5. This is that memory is spread around many parts of the brain. Invariably, the more parts of the brain that are involved in learning a

Table 4.1

	Learned skills		
	Unstructured (Instinctive – no adult help needed)	*Semi-structured* (Adult help is needed but it cannot be totally structured)	*Structured* (Can be learned by trial-and-error methods but most efficiently achieved by structured methods given by experts)
Artistic	High visual ability	Perspective, pro-portion, parallax	Primary and secondary colours Knowledge of various media
Social	Smiling	Telling a joke	Hosting a 'chat show' on TV
Musical	Perfect pitch	Ability to play an instrument	Writing an orchestral score
Linguistic	Cooing and gurgling	Talking (in one language) Talking (in more than one language)	Writing good prose Acquiring several other languages

task, however abstract, the better the memory.

In order to round off the preceding two sections and introduce the next on structured learning we can summarize some of the main features of all three types of learning by means of Table 4.1.

One of the most interesting entries in the above table is the centre one of the artistic skill range. Most normal people can be taught a laboured form of perspective and proportion in a structured way but only relatively few people will sketch using perspective with any facility. Like all the skills in the semi-structured column there is a certain air of mystery about how they are acquired. Throughout all human history until the Renaissance nobody consciously 'saw' with any sense of perspective. After it *every* artist was fully aware of perspective (even if, like the 'primitives' of today, they do not use it).

4.3 CONCEPTUAL SKILLS AND STRUCTURED LEARNING

It is highly probable that, at the microscopic level in the human brain, there is no essential difference between unstructured, semi-structured and structured learning. All such learning involves the formation of strong links between dendrites. However, we are looking at these types of learning from the point of view as to what are the best methods of presenting learning opportunities to the learner. In the case of unstructured learning we are saying that we (as teachers) are not needed; in the case of semi-structured learning we are needed but we don't know precisely how we teach; and in the case of structured learning we are very conscious of the ordered way in which we are presenting learning opportunities. Although there are no strict demarcation lines between the three categories, they help us to appreciate the differences that occur between the abilities of different individuals. This categorization will also help us to appreciate that CAL only lends itself to structured learning.

Structured learning is characteristic of the human species. There are one or two examples of animal learning that appear to be structured, though it is hard to be sure. Young chimpanzees will learn, from their mothers, how to fashion small sticks in order to poke out ants from their nests. But it is not certain that the mothers are consciously teaching the skill. By and large, we are safe in saying that the human species differs from all others in our ability to consciously analyse and structure the information and skills we gain in our lifetime so that we can hand them on before we die.

Our ability to teach in this way probably matured about 50000 years ago when our brain capacity reached its full size. From then onwards, we begin to gain evidence that something quite different began to occur in our species that had to do with concepts, theories and methodically taught skills. Neolithic people began to be buried with garlands of flowers. Later, they were buried with small orifices near their heads as though those who remained thought that they were still speaking to them. There need to be no mystical or religious explanations for this widespread behaviour. People who have lost loved ones often hear their voices after death. A hunting tribe which has lost a wise and brilliant leader could well make his advice 'permanent' by burying him in such a way. This has been discussed recently in a brilliant book by Julian Jaynes [16].

Then again, there are religious motives ascribed to cave paintings, though there is a much simpler educational reason. Cave paintings, such as those at Lascaux, are just as likely to be visual aids used by the adult members of the tribe in teaching animal anatomy or hunting techniques to the youngsters.* Another human skill which has existed for thousands of years is the making of flint spear-heads. Recently, an American anthropologist took it upon himself to acquire the skill. He could only do so by trial and error methods, of course, because there is no-one left who could teach him. It took him many months before he acquired the skill. This skill would surely have been taught by careful guidance.

We have already given an example of the first recorded case of structured teaching – the geometry dialogue between Socrates and Plato – and it is likely that this tradition had existed for several generations before that in Greek

* I am indebted for this observation to Reinet Fremlin.

culture. However, we must now leave the area of speculation.

As already mentioned in Chapter 1, there has been a considerable growth in research into the effective conditions for learning. Thousands of books on the subject must have been published in the post-war years. From these have emerged résumés, and from these even further summaries. Four broad rules appear to be important. At a general level these are the only rules that any teacher need remember. As we shall see, CAL is able to incorporate all these rules also. These rules summarize all that we have been discussing in the earlier chapters of this book. Also, modern physiological research is revealing the detailed mechanisms of learning and memory as they occur in the brain. A schema of these is given in Chapter 5. We now turn to the four general conditions.

4.3.1 Active engagement by the student

The importance of this can hardly be exaggerated. As shown in Chapter 5, the learning of any task, or any new concept, involves the laying down of a new, permanent network of interconnected neurones in the higher reaches of the brain. No network in our brain, however, is an entity isolated from the outside world. In its formation it needs both the constant stimulation of new data coming in *and* an opportunity to carry out active rehearsals as the network is shaping up. The brain evolved not just to ponder on the eternal verities but to act as a constant provider of safe strategies in real life as we meet different contingencies. Therefore, if at all possible, students should be given active opportunities to respond as they learn, even if the subject matter is mathematics or logic or a great many other things which don't appear to have much connection with everyday life.

Unless this physical exit route is provided learning does not occur. We have already mentioned the case of the kitten who watched vertical lines in a passive way. The same applies to human students. No matter how well someone *appears* to be learning something (by nods of the head and so on) it is highly likely that it will be forgotten very quickly unless opportunities are given for much more positive and active ways of responding.

It might be objected that we all know that we can learn quite adequately from sitting quietly, reading a book. This may often be so. But, invariably in these cases, the 'master' network has already been laid down in our brain. Reading from a book only modifies an existing network. And, in any case, the brain actually *does* rehearse physical activity in such cases by sending microscopic messages to our muscles. The larynx at least will be working subvocally, and probably several more muscles, too. But if we are reading totally new material from a book we greatly enhance the possibility of learning new information if we carry out overt physical activity by taking notes, or making drawings and so on. Generally speaking, the newer the material we are attempting to learn the more physical activity is required in order to establish the exit route from the new network being laid down.

There have been many technological tools brought into schools and colleges in the last 100 years or so, though it has usually taken decades for every single one of them to be accepted by teachers. The lantern slide took a generation and so did the overhead projector. In fact, none of the technological aids, until the microcomputer, made much difference at all to the effectiveness of the teaching process. The reason is quite simple: the students remain just as passive as in many other forms of classroom teaching. Research has shown that the normal rate of retention of new facts taught by old fashioned lecturing methods is about 10%. Attractive colourful slides on an overhead projector, or a film, increase retentiveness to something like 20 to 30%. This is hardly a significant increase compared with the majority of information which is totally forgotten. Retentiveness doesn't rise to 80 or 90% unless the student is actively and constantly responding. This makes the microcomputer unique and in a class of its own as a technological tool in education.

For the moment, the main form of physical response is by means of typing an answer to a question or constructing a response to a frame. As discussed in Chapter 1 there will ultimately be many other modes of responding than by typing alone. But even typing is enough to lay down those necessary exit routes from the new brain network in the course of learning.

4.3.2 Immediate reinforcement

This has already been discussed at some length and only needs reiterating at this stage. In the early days of learning anything new, reinforcement from the outside world is absolutely necessary in order to strengthen the first feeble pathways being laid down in the brain – the data lines to the new network, the new network itself and the exit routes from it. Later on, when the new network has been fairly well established, the learner starts to supply his own (unconscious) reinforcement. Once again, further discussion of this fascinating topic, together with the importance of the *immediacy* of reinforcement is given in the next chapter.

All we need to say now is that the microcomputer once again fits the bill as a uniquely new technological tool in the educational process. No other educational aid hitherto has supplied reinforcement to the individual student. And, of course, the microcomputer can supply reinforcement immediately after the learner's active response.

4.3.3 Organization of subject matter into small steps

James Watson's account of the discovery of the helical structure of DNA gave a graphic picture of the way in which he and Francis Crick stumbled through many vague, and sometimes ridiculous, ideas before they arrived at the real concept [17]. Many other lesser scientists were appalled by this disclosure of the scientific method. It gave entirely the wrong picture of what science is all about! But Watson and Crick's method was much nearer the reality than the fiction of the scientist arriving at a theory by logical deduction. The whole process of human discovery is of the successive refinement of ideas from amorphous shapeless things to concepts of great clarity.

Unfortunately, text-book writers tend to rewrite scientific history. They usually present the highly crystallized ideas first. The first sentence of any chapter often starts with a rule, or a theory or a highly polished definition. Those should really come at the end of a chapter when the author has gradually polished and shaped the learner's rough ideas.

Whenever possible, a CAL program should try to recreate a concept in the same order in which it was formed. That is, from the general to the particular. However, it is not always possible or appropriate. In these cases, substitute another rule: work from the simple to the complex. This may mean the simple addition of one fact to another and then another in a long stream as is shown in the frames in Appendix 1. At the end of this exemplary Unit the learner will not yet have reached a comprehensive understanding of the plant and animal cell but he is well on his way with the support of some well-learned facts.

Whether the CAL writer proceeds from the general to the particular, or additively, he has to organize his material beforehand in order to know exactly what he is doing at every step. In the first case it will be by successive discriminations and refinements; in the second case, by binding one piece of information to another. At every stage, *one* new learning skill is being acquired. Before a CAL Unit is started, all the intended new skills must be laid out in some organized way. This will be taken up further in Section 8.1, Task analysis.

4.3.4 Effective learning is self-paced

Everybody has different attributes, different learning speeds and different pre-existing long term memories in his brain before a new learning task is attempted. There is a natural, effective learning speed for everyone. In addition, we all have our own unique attentiveness rhythms which regularly rise and fall every 90 minutes or so. Therefore, an ideal learning system should be able to pace itself to the requirements of the student. And this, of course, is exactly what the microcomputer allows the learner to do.

5

Brain processes of learning and memory

5.1 THE NEOCORTEX

Neocortex (Fig. 5.1) means 'new skin' and the term refers to the fact that this is the most recently acquired part of animal and human brains. The important nerve cells of the neocortex, the *cortical neurones*, lie in a tissue thin layer about five to seven neurones thick. The cortical neurones are actually grouped into 'barrels' each having a diameter of about the same size as a full stop on this page, and a depth of 2 to 3 millimetres. In Fig. 5.2, where we show networks of neurones, the points are actually barrels, but for our purposes we don't need to distinguish between single neurones and barrels. Each barrel consists of several thousand neurones and can be considered to be the equivalent of a microcomputer in its computational power. There are hundreds of millions of such barrels tightly packed together over the surface neocortex. Out of each barrel comes a relatively small number of very thin hair-like *dendrites* covered with insulation. These collect in large bundles under the barrels and lead away to other parts of the brain. Sometimes these bundles straddle the left and right halves of the brain and sometimes they lead deep into the interior of the brain where other, older centres of the brain are to be found. Within the barrels each

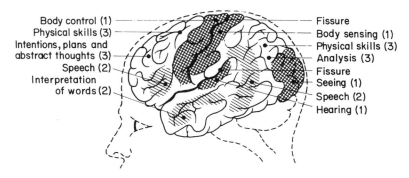

Fig. 5.1 The neocortex (new brain)

neurone has many hundreds, perhaps thousands of dendrites and these (almost) interconnect with other dendrites on other neurones. For the most part, barrels of neurones act as semi-autonomous units: that is, they are capable of a lot of independent processing before sending their results 'downstream' into the insulated bundles. There is little doubt that barrels communicate (or tentatively communicate) with one another by a sort of very high frequency 'ripple' across the top surface of the barrels. This occurs over the whole of the surface of the neocortex. This process is extremely important. As animals evolved, and indeed as we evolved from *homo erectus* and earlier species, it was this surface layer of the neocortex that was expanding successively from species to species. If we look at the neocortices of mammals whose development became largely stabilized millions of years ago we find that their brains are smoothly surfaced. The cat's neocortex is quite smooth except for one or two large folds. But as we go from one mammal to a 'higher' one in the evolutionary league table, we find that their brains, besides getting larger (relative to body size), also became more wrinkled. Our brains are the wrinkliest of all. Indeed, large parts of our cortex have been pushed down into deep cracks or fissures. You can see two of these fissures in Fig. 5.1.

The 'rippling' that goes on between the surface neurones of the barrels, whether the surface is inside a wrinkle or fissure or not, is the method by which new communications and new learning are established. Precisely how this happens is still one of the greatest mysteries of the brain. One of the greatest brain physiologists in the world, Sir John Eccles, who is a strong Christian and therefore believes in the soul and free-will, believes that one's 'spiritual self' plays upon the surface of the neocortex and decides which barrels should be receptive and which should not. But very few brain specialists accept this and prefer to leave the question open for the time being until more is known about this rippling, or beta brain-wave, activity.

The neocortices of early mammals consisted mainly of the *primary sensory* areas of the brain, marked (1) in Fig. 5.1. But as we go from one mammalian species to a higher one, the neocortical surface in between gets larger and larger and the primary areas get pushed down into deep fissures. In the case of man, the surface in between, the 'inter-sensory' or *polysensory* areas, have become quite large. Indeed, when visual, hearing or bodily messages reach the primary areas for processing, they tend to ripple outwards into the polysensory areas. Parts of the polysensory areas can, in fact, have quite precise functions. These are marked (2) in Fig. 5.1. The front one marked 'speech' lies near the neurones of the primary sensory area to do with moving the lips and the larynx. If the speech (2) area is destroyed in someone who has a stroke, then that person cannot pronounce words. The speech (2) area lying near the hearing (1) area deals with grammar and syntax. If someone has a stroke in this area, he can pronounce words readily enough but cannot speak in sentences that make any sense. The polysensory areas marked with a (3) are the most interesting and mysterious of the lot because they are the areas that are characteristically much larger in humans than other animals. The front region is undoubtedly to do with abstract thought, intentions and plans (and where our most complex 'theories' lie) but there is much to be learned yet.

5.2 LONG-TERM MEMORY

For most purposes, all the adjacent barrels of the neocortex can be considered to be weakly in touch with one another. A long-term memory of a particular idea or skill can be considered to be a network of particular neurones that cover the *whole* of the neocortex like an incredibly fine piece of Nottingham lace. That is, each network can be considered to consist of thousands, perhaps millions, of *major* interconnections between the neurones (barrels) of the neocortex. In between the network are hundreds of millions of barrels which, largely, do not get involved when the idea or skill network becomes activated. The 'mesh' of the network is not uniformly spread over the surface but will be dense in some areas and dispersed in others. All networks of ideas or skills will have at least two areas of fine mesh, one in the body control (1) area and one in another of the primary sensory areas. Imagine now, hundreds of millions of such networks, largely autonomous, but lying incredibly intermeshed between one another all over the surface of the neocortex. Figure 5.2 shows a small part of two such networks, each point being a barrel or biological microcomputer.

You will have noticed that we have been interchanging the use of 'skills', 'words', 'ideas' and 'thoughts' as though they were all the same thing. They are, in fact. To the brain, it makes no difference what we call them: they are all the same thing. We could add some other terms like 'concepts', 'acquired habits', 'cognitive processes' and so on. They are all networks of neurones. The only qualitative difference between them is whereabouts in the brain they are more finely meshed than others. Each thought, or skill, or whatever, will

The network of two separate ideas, words, skills, thoughts. In the blank areas there are thousands of other neurones belonging to other networks

Fig. 5.2

have its own characteristic network of fine and dispersed mesh over the whole of the neocortex.

This leads us to the most important concept of all when thinking about the brain. This is that nothing in the neocortex happens in isolation. A highly abstract idea will have a network that is finely meshed somewhere in the front part of the brain but it will also have important interconnections with all other parts, too. If we think of the word 'neurone', for example, then the visual processing parts of the brain will tend to 'see' the word 'neurone', our hearing centre will 'hear' it and our bodily control centre will be sending out microscopic messages to our larynx to 'say' the word 'neurone'.

How do messages travel within the networks? They do so by means of microscopically small electrical 'spikes'. These electrical spikes travel up a dendrite, through the main central body of the neurone and then on to the end of another dendrite. When the electrical spike gets to the end of a dendrite it gets held up. There is, in fact, a gap and it is too wide for the electrical spike to jump. It has to be ferried across to the next dendrite by means of small 'packets' of chemicals called *transmitter substances*. These transmitter substances are charged up by the electrical spike and, when they get to the other side of the gap, give up their electrical charge, and the spike continues on its way up the new dendrite at high speed. The gap between adjoining dendrites is called a *synapse*. Every synapse has a store of transmitter substances lying close to the synaptic surface. As the transmitter substances are used up they are replenished from the centre of the neurone, though at a relatively slow rate.

If the transmitter substances at a synapse are heavily used, so heavily that the neurone becomes temporarily exhausted, then a major development takes place in the neurone. Over a period of several hours (assuming the neurone receives plenty of energy and food from the bloodstream) the transmitter substances are not only replaced but *new reservoirs* are laid down at the synaptic endings of the dendrites. And this is a *permanent* change. Whatever happens to the neurone after this, the enlarged stock of transmitter substances is permanent so long as the neurone remains alive. Thus, as new electrical spikes or messages, come into the neocortex they either travel along existing major networks, already furnished with large synaptic reservoirs, or they cause new ones to be established. Examples of the former would include practising a long-perfected skill or remembering your telephone number; an example of the latter would be the news that the goolongs on Venus are becoming restless. If you didn't know this then I had better explain that goolongs are rather squat, not to say squashy and incredibly ugly creatures, that live on the surface of Venus. They wear green high-pressure suits rather like deep-sea divers. In learning this amazing new fact, some of the neurones in your neocortex are becoming drained. If I were to ask you to write the word 'goolong' and, even more so, to draw a few goolongs (in lurid green), then the publishers of this book and I would be in danger of being sued by you for causing permanent structural change of an entirely worthless nature in your neocortex. For the goolong neurones concerned would spend the next several hours laying down large permanent stocks of transmitter substances at new synaptic junctions. In fact, I am in danger of doing so already, so I won't mention the word '. . . . . . .' again!

Now the networks of thoughts/habits/concepts/skills/facts/words/abstractions and so on in the neocortex have to be activated by electrical impulses coming from evolutionary older parts of the brain. Not only this, but the networks have to have exit routes, too, to the older parts of the brain and then to the body. Even the most abstract thought (that is, a whole–brain network which is very finely meshed in the front of the brain) has some bodily effects, however minute. Long-term memory is therefore a sort of central pivot between the data that is sent from the old brain and resultant behaviour that is performed in or by the body. Let us first look at the part of the old brain that sends the data in.

5.3 SHORT-TERM MEMORY

Long-term memory networks in the neocortex take several hours to lay down. This is because hundreds, perhaps thousands, of neurones have got to replenish transmitter substances and then lay down new permanent stocks. This can only be done if the new networks are sufficiently exhausted by repeated electrical spikes or impulses from the old brain. They originate, in fact, from a curiously-shaped region called the *hippocampus* (Fig. 5.3). When new information is received from the eyes, ears, bodily senses, etc. it is routed, via the *thalamus* (which you can liken to a telephone exchange) to the hippocampus. The hippocampus is the site of the *short-term* memory. There have been a few distressing cases of people who have suffered injury to the hippocampus. They can remember new facts by assiduously repeating them to themselves as we do when we want to temporarily remember a telephone

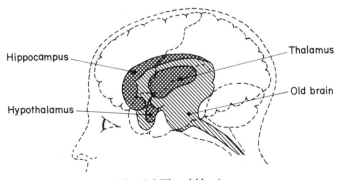

Fig. 5.3 The old brain

number. By very strenuous effort they might be able to remember new facts for a few minutes. But, as soon as their attention is directed elsewhere, this *very* short term memory (or *iconic* memory) is forgotten. This is because the new facts never get into the hippocampus.

The hippocampus is a sort of probation centre. Its purpose is to retain new data for long enough to consider whether they are significant and worth remembering permanently. During the day, in fact, a great deal of new information enters the hippocampus but it is never remembered. It slips away in reverie or when we dream at night. The brain decides that it is junk and gets rid of it. Indeed, we forget far more than we remember and the brain is a great 'forgetter' rather than 'rememberer'.

The hippocampus has a characteristic biological rhythm by which it sends out regular radar-like impulses to the neocortex. If any new information has any connection with long-term memory already in the neocortex then the hippocampus becomes much more sensitized to it. If no connection can be found then the new information is in great danger of being placed in the 'to be forgotten' compartment of the hippocampus. Its significance, however, can be greatly enhanced if other new information, closely associated with it, is also introduced into the hippocampus at about the same time. The new information can be temporarily linked together and the new complex is then 'offered' to some part of a network in the neocortex. Maybe the second lot of information finds some link. What happens then is that the hippocampus will repeatedly radiate this new information to the neocortex over a period of hours until a new network, or perhaps an important, partial, subsidiary network is established in the new brain.

But there might be instances when quite a cluster of brand new and richly associated information comes into the hippocampus, is offered to the neocortex, but is not taken up by any network. The danger then is that the whole cluster of new information might be forgotten. One way in which the new information can be retained in this case is by frequent repetition. If the new information is repeatedly forced into the hippocampus then, after about 10 to 15 minutes, the hippocampus becomes so sensitized to it that it will sweep the information into the neocortex much more persistently. Even the most remote, vaguest association that can be found in the neocortex will then be used as a 'hook' on which to hang a new network. If you are learning anything particularly novel, this 15 minutes 'warm-up' period is very important. This is why learning is often hard work. But after this 'warm-up' period, the new information begins to register in the neocortex and then successive bouts of new information find welcoming (albeit new) networks in the brain. Even the most boring subject can become interesting if persistent attention is paid to it for at least 10 to 15 minutes.

The hippocampus has to resist new information because, otherwise, it would go straight into the neocortex. It would not be long before the neocortex would become a total 'white-out' like an overexposed photograph. But we have still not adequately explained how the hippocampus decides whether a piece of new information is really significant. We have said that repeated bouts of new information over a period of about 15 minutes will cause the hippocampus to be persistent in getting it into the neocortex. But repetition, by itself, is probably not enough. Indeed, the brain is very adept at shutting off repeated, but very similar new information, before it gets to the hippocampus. This is called *habituation*. For example, if you started to work in a room with a very loud clock its noise might initially annoy you. But within a very short time you would not hear it. Or rather, your ears would hear it, but some neurones would cut the message before it reached the hippocampus.

If someone experiences new information in the environment it is likely to become significant if he *attends* to it. This does not mean passive contemplation. It involves an *active* enquiry. A cat coming across a new object will tap it this way and that way with its paws. Looking at new information from different angles and with different associations will ensure that it will not be habituated to and will be allowed through to the hippocampus.

Some new information, however, can be so important for our well-being and knowledge of the world that even *one* exposure to it can allow it straight through the hippocampus into the neocortex. The rather leisurely 15 minutes dalliance in the hippocampus won't do at all. For example, the first time that we accidentally strike a match and burn ourselves, the memory becomes well enough engraved in our minds for us never to repeat the accident. Yet the single new experience led to a long-term network.

The emotion of the pain acted as a powerful wave which swept its way through all the intervening parts of the brain, carrying the information with it. This is where we now turn to another important part of our brain.

5.4 THE HYPOTHALAMUS: THE PLEASURE/PAIN CENTRE

We have already shown, in Fig. 5.3, where the hypothalamus is situated. It is, in fact, just a little way above the roof of your mouth. If you hold a very cold piece of ice against the roof of your mouth with your tongue then you can produce some very strange bodily feelings because the hypothalamus has some very powerful effects over many processes of the body and mind. The hypothalamus is where the 'power wave' of pain originates. And the effect of this power wave is called *reinforcement*. It reinforces the feeble effect made by the new information alone. It makes the new information highly significant, even though it only occurred once.

Let us teach a student a new fact by this method. We take a swishy piece of cane, the sort that Victorian schoolmasters used to love. We hide it behind our back so as not to make the student nervous. We then ask him: 'What is the state capital of Australia?' He doesn't know, so we tell him. Or, better still, because we want to make sure his attention is fully occupied, we tell him to write it. Just as he finishes 'Canberra', his eyes still glued to the paper, we give him the most almighty whack with the cane. He leaps out of the chair in pain, of course. But he will never forget 'Canberra' – not for the whole of his lifetime. 'Canberra' will be safely lodged as a new network in his neocortex, probably as a subsidiary network of what he already knows about Australia.

What an excellent method of teaching! Yes, it would be if that were the only fact we wanted to teach him that morning. It would not be if you wanted to go on and teach him other facts. The hypothalamus, besides sending out a power wave to the neocortex, which carried 'Canberra' with it, also sets in train other events in the body. These are collectively known as the 'flight or fight' response. Powerful hormones would be sent out by the pituitary and adrenalin glands to repair the damage. His body would be immediately geared up to escape. He would be anxious and highly stressed. In short, he is no longer in a fit state to learn anything for quite some time. In any case, the information that was carried so efficiently to the neocortex probably also included his perceptions of you. You would be associated in his mind with possible punishment.

But how much better it would be if another 'power wave' of pleasure, rather than pain, could be sent out from the hypothalamus. It, too, could reinforce learning new information. It so happens that the hypothalamus can do this. In everyday parlance, the hypothalamus is known as the *pleasure/pain centre*. Within the space of a few millimetres there are to be found the sites of the most powerful pains *and* pleasures that it is possible to feel. The sites are so close within the hypothalamus that some brain scientists believe that it is the same group of cells responsible for both feelings, and that it simply depends in which direction the electrical impulse flows. Only a small number of people have ever experienced these hypothalamic feelings in their complete, 'pure' form. This has only happened by accident when a brain surgeon has been probing gently for a tumour or for some other serious purpose. The feeling of pleasure has been described as 'not sexual as such, but like a series of orgasms'. In the case of laboratory animals, the pleasure is so great that they will work at a task in order to be stimulated. This can be done by passing brief, microscopic electric currents through the pleasure region. They will work so hard, in fact, that they will not stop to eat or drink until they drop down exhausted. On revival they will continue to work until they drop dead. So the 100%, complete pleasure feeling from the hypothalamus is the most powerful motivator that it is possible to have. If, however, the microelectrode had been placed only a few millimetres away then the opposite feeling of the most intense punishment would result. A human subject has described this feeling as the most overwhelming feeling of anguish, beyond the power of description.

The scientist who discovered the pleasure/pain centre, the hypothalamus, was an American, James Olds. Tragically, his life was cut short in the middle of a brilliant career. However, he did write a book on his findings, the details of which are to be found in the Recommended bibliography.

In real life, the full totality of the feelings of pain or pleasure are not experienced. We only experience partial pain or pleasure. And these, too, are associated with other feelings from the body. So the feelings of pleasure from sex, eating, drinking and so on, which we think are different are, in fact, from the same source. The same applies to partial feelings of pain that occur when we do things that are injurious to the body or, in some cases (e.g. guilt in breaking a religious commandment), when we do things that one of the networks in our neocortex thinks is wrong. These partial feelings of pain or pleasure motivate most of our activities in our daily lives.

Therefore, if 'pleasure power waves' can be created when new information is being acquired, then it is likely that such new information will be powerfully swept through the hippocampus to the neocortex. And this is precisely what can be done. This is what the behavioural scientists of the 1950s discovered. They called this power wave 'reinforcement', not pleasure, because at the time they had no means of measuring or knowing what pleasure was scientifically. But we know now, so there is no reason why reinforcement should also not be called pleasure or reward and still remain scientific. So if we teach a dog a new trick and reward him immediately with a biscuit, then we make it more certain that the new trick will not be forgotten but retained in his neocortex. If we repeatedly reward him after several of the new tricks we can be very certain that a new permanent network will be established.

There is no reason why a CAL microcomputer should not have a small compartment containing sweets or small coins which could be dispensed one by one every time a new fact is correctly acquired! (Though this sort of training is, in fact, done – without micros, of course – in mental hospitals for retraining people with strange behaviour.) A far better sort of reward is 'knowledge of results'. That is, we have new information before us, or we have just performed a new skill, and then we are rewarded with the knowledge of the result. There are, in fact, quite strong dendritic pathways between even the most abstract, 'intellectual' areas of the neocortex and the hypothalamus. This was an epochal discovery by one of James Olds's students, Aryeh Routtenberg, in the 1970s. Intellectual knowledge of results is, in fact, as fully a 'natural' reward to the brain as any of our more basic satisfactions. There is a lot of confusion in some educators' minds as to whether 'correct' results or 'incorrect' results are better for reinforcement, or even a mixture of both. This matter obscures a lot of the debate in the field of CAL. For this reason this question is separately discussed in Section 3.7, Incorrect responses.

5.5 A PARADIGM OF LEARNING AND MEMORY

We are now in a position to present a complete paradigm of what happens when new facts are learned, or new skills acquired or when old mental concepts are reshaped into new ones. The paradigm is shown as a series of six steps in Fig. 5.4. The paradigm, it must be noted, is a simplified account of what occurs. A great number of additional and subsidiary mental processes are also involved, but the paradigm covers all the essential steps that the CAL writer needs to know. The hippocampus and the hypothalamus, which are normally to be found tucked inside the covering of the neocortex, have been separated in the figure for clarity.

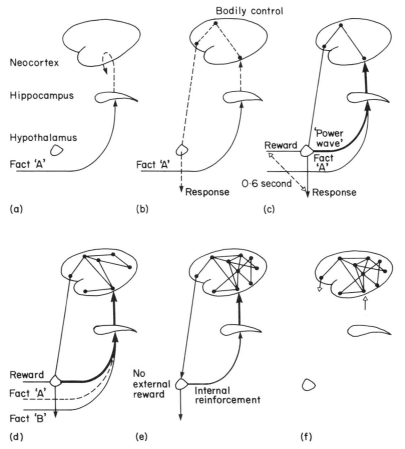

Fig. 5.4 (a) Passive reception; (b) active response; (c) reinforcement; (d) association, shaping or discrimination; (e) consolidation: (f) long–term memory

(a) Passive reception

Figure 5.4(a) supposes that a new piece of information enters the hippocampus. It has not been reinforced in any way so it is held there extremely tentatively. It is sent to the neocortex in the course of the usual consultation process which regularly goes on between these two parts of the brain. However, the fact concerned is not received and remains in the hippocampus.

(b) Active response

In this case we ask the student to make an active response to the new fact. Even if it is just a matter of copying a word then an initial rudimentary track is made in the neocortex. This is far from being a network of any significance, but it's a start. You will notice (Fig. 5.4(b)) that the pathway goes to the region of the neocortex concerned with bodily control. You will also notice that the exit route appears to pass through the hypothalamus. The commands to the fingers to type the response or to the larynx to say the word will not, in fact, pass through the hypothalamus. But it is *always* informed of any activity resulting from a neocortical network. It should not be thought of as any sort of controller, but it certainly acts as a powerful 'referee'. And the hypothalamus is a very versatile referee, too. By virtue of the fact that the hypothalamus controls the master gland of the body, the pituitary, it acts like a referee who sits on the fence that divides the mind from the body. The hypothalamus not only reacts to, sometimes, extremely delicate, highly abstract thought processes in the brain, but also to very basic autonomic physiological processes in the body, such as hunger, thirst, body temperature and a great deal else besides. In fact, by its very nature the notion that the body and mind are separate entities cannot now be sustained (at least by most of those who study the subject).

(c) Reinforcement

We now suppose that, as soon as the student has given a response, the microcomputer (or human tutor) rewards him by confirming that the answer was correct. This time, as you can see from Fig. 5.4(c), a 'pleasure power wave' leaves the hypothalamus and follows the same track as the original pathway. The delay between the response and the reinforcement appears to be highly important, and it is 0.6 second. This time delay is called *latency*. Its importance has to do with the recovery time that is needed by the neurones that were initially activated. As soon as a message is ferried across a synapse by the transmitter substances the surface layer of the dendrite is temporarily exhausted. Other reservoirs of transmitter substances have to move into place right at the very edge of the synapse. This takes 0.6 second. If the power wave comes sooner than this then the neurone is not ready to transmit. However, if the reward or reinforcement is delayed much beyond a few seconds then the neurone pathway largely disappears. The process is a little like a lightning strike. Initially, there is a rather weak ionization track that leaves the charged cloud and hits the earth. Almost immediately a powerful return stroke of lightning leaves the earth and returns along the ionization track. Much the same appears to happen in the case of reinforcement in the brain.

It has already been remarked that, in normal everyday life, the intensities of the pleasure and pain waves from the hypothalamus rarely correspond to those discovered in brain surgery. This means that, even with reinforcement, a new fact or experience is not often engraved in the neocortex in one shot, as would occur with a sudden, terrifying emergency like our previous examples of a matches accident or being whacked by a cane. Experience from both animal learning experiments and from PL and CAL is that a new fact or skill needs to be reinforced for at least six times before it can be assumed that it is being laid down in permanent memory. This is a good working rule. A great deal of judgement has to be used by the CAL writer when first introducing a new fact. If it is a difficult concept, or has a difficult spelling, then it may need to be repeated (in different contexts, if possible) a dozen times or more. This will be revealed, of couse, when the CAL program is tested. Anyway, as we leave Fig 5.4(c) let us assume that fact 'A' has been reinforced by itself two or three times. At this stage, although it is not yet securely lodged in the neocortex, it is useful, to avoid boredom and possible habituation, to associate it with other facts, or to refine it in some way.

(d) Association, shaping or discrimination

In Fig. 5.4(d), fact 'B' has been introduced, responded to, and reinforced. This fact 'B' can be a separate fact closely related to 'A', or it can be a refinement or careful discrimination of 'A', or it can be a subsequent 'shaping' of a general skill introduced as 'A'. Whatever this second stage is, the result, as you can see from the diagram, is a more complex network.

(e) Consolidation

We have already mentioned that, if reinforcement is gradually withdrawn at a late stage in learning, the subject becomes conditioned not to expect a reward *every* time a response has been made. Rewards are still expected and so the student starts to learn persistence. This helps the student to remain motivated even after completing a program. What actually happens within the brain is that the 'knowledge of results' – the firm down arrow leading from the neocortex (Fig. 5.4(e)) – causes the hypothalamus to continue sending out confirmatory power waves without the need for external reinforcement. However, this should only be done when the new cluster of facts or the desired skill level has been fully assimilated in the neocortex. This continues to consolidate the new network.

(f) Long-term memory

Figure 5.4(f) represents a fully established new network. The two small arrows represent the fact that this network now has the potential to receive data and to express itself in activity. It is not, as it were, an independent thought or skill or concept. There would be no way of knowing whether such a network existed in the neocortex until it were stimulated and then the resultant behaviour observed. This is one interesting difference between a microcomputer and a brain. By careful examination of all the circuits in a microcomputer, its performance can be accurately anticipated. It would be impossibly difficult to examine a brain in this way. It cannot be considered to be as hard-wired as a computer, even though long-term memory is permanent. The brain is capable of serendipity. For example, if someone is presented with some new information that has similarities with two or three separate networks then these networks are likely to interact with one another and form some intermediate bridging network between them. A computer cannot deal with ambiguous information like this. It's more of an open or shut business: a computer will either accept information that it is precisely programmed for or it will reject it.

6
The structure of the CAL Unit

6.1 THE CAL UNIT

The term Unit is reserved for the set of frames that a student will comfortably complete in one study session. CAL programs do not really come into their own until the student is about 11 or 12 years old and ready for those subjects that need structured learning. Schools usually block off the day into periods of between 40 and 60 minutes and this seems sensible.

Indeed, there is evidence that 40 to 60 minutes is a suitable session for a person of any age. There are many different sorts of brain rhythms which are characteristic of a healthy person. Some pulsations occur many times a second and emanate from specialized centres inside the brain such as the thalamus or the one already mentioned as being important for memory, the hippocampus. Other pulsations occur on a daily basis; others on a monthly basis. An even longer one is associated with the amount of daylight a person receives and so is on a yearly cycle. The one that concerns us here is the 'attention' cycle, a pulsation that emanates from a nerve centre in the higher reaches of the neck called the *reticular formation*. This is a 90 minute cycle. In other words, the human brain passes from peak attention efficiency down to a low ebb 45 minutes later, and then back again to high attention 45 minutes later still. So a learning session will be ideal if it can be timed to start on a rising curve of attention, then passing through peak attention, and then stopping before the attention curve gets too low.

6.2 NUMBER OF FRAMES

In the immediate future, most CAL Units will probably be used in schools, though in the longer term CAL is likely to be used by people working on their home micros. So, for both school reasons and for the physiological reasons mentioned above, a 40 to 60 minute Unit seems the best. How many frames such a session will need depends very much on the nature of the material. In the early stages of a new subject, fairly simple concepts or facts are being presented and the density of the material in each frame will be low. Typically, such a

Unit will have a large number of frames, perhaps as many as 150 to 170. In the higher reaches of a subject quite lengthy passages may be presented on the screen and requiring a lot of thought. There might also be lengthy calculations. In such cases, a Unit may only consist of a few dozen frames.

No general rule can be laid down. The CAL writer must make an initial judgement about the number, and modify this if necessary after the pilot trial. Usually a new CAL writer will find that a large number of additional frames will have to be written after the trial. It can be a hit or miss affair for a while until the writer gets used to the subject matter.

As already discussed, aim to break down a subject into the smallest assimilable step size, given the grade of student taking the course.

6.3 SUMMARY OF FRAME TYPES

Before we move on to discussing the structure of a CAL Unit let us remind ourselves of the four principal frame types that we have met:

1. *I-frames* Introduction-frames are those which introduce new facts, skills or concepts for the first time. There are likely to be few of these in a Unit.
2. *T-frames* These immediately follow I-frames. Usually there needs to be only one T-frame after each I-frame, but sometimes, when the fact or concept is a difficult one, there might be a series of T-frames, each progressively less cued.
3. *L-frames* When new facts or concepts have made an initial lodgement in the student's hippocampus after introduction and testing, they are linked together with other material as quickly as possible. This is where the creativity of the CAL writer is really tested in looking for as many different, relevant associations as possible and, of course, enriching the frame if the subject matter is austere. This is where the real hard work is done – both by the writer and the student!
4. *FT-frames* Final test-frames. They are totally uncued, often not reinforced and are the final confirmation that the CAL writer has done his job well. If the subject is an examined one, a CAL Unit, whenever possible, should contain actual examination questions or parts of them. Where there is not an examination at the end of the course, the CAL writer should supply specific, realistic and measurable educational objectives for each Unit (see Chapter 8 for more on this). The FT-frames test these objectives.

6.4 THE STRUCTURE OF A CAL UNIT

We have already mentioned that new information entering the brain is sent to the hippocampus for temporary storage. From there the new information is offered to the neocortex for linking purposes. There is, in fact, a continual consulatation process going on between the hippocampus and the neocortex, a thin tissue covering the outside surface of the brain in which layers of neurones record permanent memory networks. If the new information does not match or seem to have any sort of relationship with existing networks in the neocortex, then it remains in the hippocampus. More often than not, this new information loses its potency and dies away. Much of this information is also swept away at night during dreaming.

If, however, this new information is vigorously reinforced and worked on actively by the student for about 15 minutes or so then the hippocampus becomes 'sensitized' to it and becomes much more insistent that a lodgement is found somewhere in the neocortex. The receptivity of the new – but tentatively learned – information in the hippocampus can be enhanced enormously if it can be associated with material that the student has already acquired, perhaps from a previous CAL Unit. After this period of about 15 minutes the new information starts to lay down new networks in the neocortex. Not only this but the hippocampus will repeatedly send it back again to the neocortex until the latter has well and truly established new networks.

Let us assume that six new facts are separately introduced into the hippocampus in the first 15 minutes of a CAL Unit by means of repeated responses and reinforcements. The hippocampus, in turn, offers these six separate facts to the neocortex. Let us also assume that, after all this hard work, only one fact makes a fragile connection with something vaguely similar in the neocortex. The student then stops his CAL session and goes to dig in the garden and speak to his neighbour over the fence. The result of this will be that only the one fact will be repeatedly offered to the neocortex over the next few hours. The other five will not be taken up and will then be forgotten by the hippocampus in the usual way. The sixth fact is likely to be remembered.

In actuality, such an instance is highly improbable though we could think of an example that might be near the mark: let us say, a CAL Unit teaching six Tibetan words with unusual spellings and all quite novel to the learner. By chance, one of them was somewhat similar to a botanical term that the student had learned in a CAL Unit the previous day. Even though the student was not conscious of the connection it was, in fact, the reason why this particular Tibetan word found a lodgement. However, if the CAL writer who'd written the Tibetan Unit had also richly associated *all* the words together during the program there would have been a better chance of the other five words being pulled through into the neocortex. There would have been a much higher chance if the CAL writer had put in other sorts of associations with facts likely to be known by the student.

This account of memory formation, simplified though it is, leads on to two extremely important rules in structuring CAL Units:

1. If the new information in a CAL Unit is likely to be completely novel to the student and there appear to be no likely associations with existing material, then it should be introduced *as early as possible* in the program. This will give plenty of opportunities to the writer to form new associations, both between the new facts and between them and other material which the student is likely to have in his neocortex.

2. If the new information is likely to have strong associations with knowledge already well known to the student then it can be introduced in a more regular way throughout the Unit. However, it is still useful to ensure that nothing new appears in the last 15 minutes or so of the Unit to ensure that plenty of practice takes place then. This more regular introduction also applies to concept shaping. If the student starts off with a vague, but well-understood concept then it will already be securely lodged in his neocortex. As it is shaped and discriminated and refined in the course of the Unit it is highly likely that all the steps, even up until quite late stages of the Unit, will be safely pulled through into his neocortex.

Now it is impossible, of course, that a CAL writer will know what is already in a student's mind before he starts a Unit. He must make some assumptions from what he can guess about the experience and abilities of the student. If the writer gets things badly wrong it will always be revealed during testing. It is much easier for the CAL writer if he is writing a long series of Units in a course. He can then be very sure about what foundations he is building on at every stage.

Figures 6.1–6.3 summarize what we have been discussing in this chapter by showing three possible shapes of the ways in which the four types of frames may be distributed within a Unit. To give some approximate guidance the

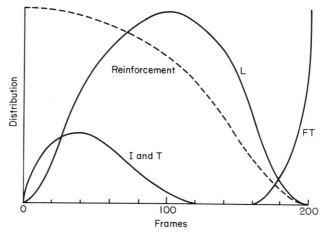

Fig. 6.1

Units shown below are all envisaged as being 200 frames long. They are not to be followed slavishly, of course. Every CAL Unit will be uniquely different.

6.5 FRONT-END LOADING

For material that is likely to be completely novel to the student, it is introduced

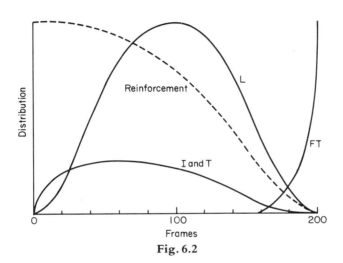

Fig. 6.2

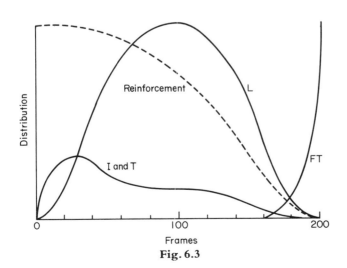

Fig. 6.3

and tested in the early part of the Unit (Fig. 6.1). Half–way through the Unit, as you can see, all the new information has been dealt with and all the frames are L–frames. The dotted line signifies that all frames are reinforced in the early part of a Unit but tail off (in a random way) towards the end.

6.6 EVEN–LOADING

Figure 6.2 for the I–frames and T–frames typifies information which is probably well known to the student but is being treated in different ways. This also applies to a readily grasped concept which is being progressively refined in the course of the Unit.

6.7 HYBRID STRUCTURES

The distribution in Fig. 6.3 is probably nearest to reality for most Units. Some brand new material is introduced very early and is then associated with other, not so novel information, during the Unit.

7
Frame formats

7.1 AUTHORING LANGUAGES AND SYSTEMS

As has been mentioned earlier in this book, it is strongly recommended that the CAL writer devotes himself to the preparation, writing and testing of CAL programs and not to coding it as well. If you are seriously contemplating writing a great deal of good CAL material then try to team up with someone who is a good programmer. As far as the CAL program is concerned, the programming language doesn't matter. At the present time, the vast majority of microcomputers for the home and school use only BASIC. But as more powerful micros come along in the future, then they'll be able to be programmed in PASCAL, COBOL, LISP, FORTH and so on.

For CAL Units that are largely textual, the demands made on the programmer are not great. However, if you use a lot of graphics, particularly if they are animated, then you will need an expert programmer – an assembly programmer. An assembly programmer will be writing in a language closer to the machine's own characteristics. The visual and animated effects obtainable from assembly coding are quicker and more spectacular than in 'higher' languages such as BASIC.

There is yet another way of coding your program and this is by going to an even higher level language, called an *authoring language*. By this method you will be able to instruct the microcomputer by means of a restricted number of quite ordinary English-like commands. If you are interested in using an authoring language do try to test one thoroughly first. Prepare a sequence of varied frames and see how the demonstrator copes – or better still, how you cope before you purchase. You will probably notice that the authoring system will restrict you to certain formats – or characteristic sorts of frames – on the screen, but you may be happy with that. Most authoring languages rely heavily, for example, on multiple choice formats and branching programs. Authoring languages vary between the pathetic and the quite brilliant, but even some of the latter have large lacunae. Bear in mind, also, that any authoring language you buy may restrict you to one particular model of a micro. Scores of authoring languages have been left behind over the years as computers improved. On the whole, I would advise waiting for another few years until microcomputers become more standardized. However, Appendix 2 lists details of some well-known examples.

Normally speaking, the CAL writer need not worry overmuch about formats. The structure of the Unit and the type of frame are much more important. The format of a frame will often be decided by the particular nature of the teaching material at that point, and the technical constraints of the microcomputer you are writing for. However, the beginner CAL writer can often become repetitious in his formats and might want to refresh himself about different ways of arranging the frame and calling for a response. This chapter can be used for this purpose. Of course, the number of possible formats will grow enormously over the coming years as the technical facilities of the normal microcomputer improve.

7.2 FRAME FORMATS

Like a good golfer who is equally adept with any of his clubs, an experienced CAL writer will move freely between many different formats. Sometimes, although the skilled CAL writer will always know what type of frame he wants to write, he cannot make up his mind about its format. When Edgar Allen Poe was stumped for an idea for a new story he would open an encyclopaedia at random and stick a pin in the page. You could do the same with the check list (section 7.17) at the end of this chapter if you wish.

7.3 NO-RESPONSE FORMAT

An example of one such has already been given in Chapter 2 (Frame 2.2). In the following we have an example of the CAL writer using a no-response format where he wants a short interlude in the program. In this case the student has learned something of plant cells. The CAL writer now wants to turn to animal cells. (Later in the Unit, he will contrast them.) So, to separate the two parts, and also to give the student a short rest and some praise, the CAL writer inserts a non-teaching, no-response frame (Frame 7.1).

All the other frames in this Unit are, of couse, response-frames.

7.4 COPY FORMAT

This is the simplest format of all. Frame 7.2 is an I-frame in a geography Unit.

Such an I-frame is, of course, extremely easy to answer. But unless the learner's attention is brought to it at this stage there is a high chance that it will be mis-spelled some time later in the Unit. This frame is also a useful way of showing, without having to state the rule, that the correct response does not always have to have the same number of letters as the dots.

Frame 7.1

Well done! You can rest here for a while if you
want. In the previous frames you have learned
the names and functions of some major features
of plant cells.

In the following frames we are going to look at
animal cells. But don't worry! It'll be no more
difficult than the previous lot, and many of the
parts are exactly the same!

When you're ready, press RETURN as usual

Frame 7.2

Students frequently spell 'Arctic' wrongly,
leaving out the first 'c'.

Type the word here.

....

Frame 7.3

E – EXCHANGE Control
S – SUBSIDIES to home industries
T – TARIFFS (Import Duties)
U
A
R
Y

Note that 'Tariffs' has one 'r' and .... 'f's.

Frame 7.3 is another very simple copy frame, though it seems more complicated at first.

Frame 7.3 also involves a mnemonic device. This is, in fact, a later frame from the same Unit mentioned in Chapter 3 with its memory grid, 'TRADES AROUND ESTUARY'. Frame 7.4 is another copy frame using 'Around' as the memory word. This is an I-frame, of course.

7.5 FADED PROMPT FORMAT

Frame 7.5 could appropriately follow the 'Tariff' frame shown previously.

Frame 7.5 is now a T-frame. It could be followed by yet another faded prompt (Frame 7.6).

Faded prompt frames are the only exception to the convention that the dots are of standard length. It would obviously be misleading to use the normal number of dots in this case. This last stage of a faded prompt is, in fact, similar to a cued format, which now follows.

7.6 CUED FORMAT

Frame 7.7 is an I-frame, of course, and very easy to respond to. But if the dots were not cued with a 'c' some students would reply with 'muscles'.

7.7 TWO-CHOICE FORMAT

The two-choice format of Frame 7.8 speaks for itself. Frame 7.9 is another variation.

Frame 7.9 develops a syllogistic-type argument which the learner has to solve without any obvious prompt being shown. This constructed response requires careful thought by the student and the CAL writer should seek plenty of opportunities of including this sort of frame in his programs. Frame 7.10 is another good example of such a frame.

Some more examples of two-choice frames are Frames 7.11–7.13.

Frame 7.11 is a T-frame: so also is Frame 7.12, a two-choice example from a bookkeeping program.

Frame 7.13, although it is a two-choice frame, is testing several facts that have been taught in previous frames. It is an L-frame.

7.8 MULTIPLE-CHOICE FORMAT

Multiple-choice frames are used occasionally in linear programs (Frame 7.14).

However, multiple-choice questions must be composed with great care. If the choices are too similar then they can easily become confusing – and may well teach a wrong response if used as an I-frame. If the choices are too

Frame 7.4

A – Avoiding overdependence on
imports of strategic goods
R
O
U
N
D

The memory word 'Around' introduces the reasons why a government might wish to restrict some parts of its international trade. Just in case there's a war in the future, a government will always want to grow as much food as possible and .... a great deal of reliance on importing food from other countries which might get cut off.

Frame 7.5

E – EXCHANGE Control
S – SUBSIDIES to home industries
T – TA . I . . S (Import Duties)
U
A
R
Y

Frame 7.6

E – EXCHANGE Control
S – SUBSIDIES to home industries
T – T . . . . . . (Import Duties)
U
A
R
Y

Frame 7.7

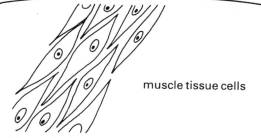

muscle tissue cells

A house is constructed from bricks.
The tissues of plants and animals are composed
of living units called c..........

Frame 7.8

The ropes
that will
have to take
the weight of
the second
climber are:

1. A and B

2. B and C

Type 1 or 2

Frame 7.9

Until 1982, microcomputers were too expensive
for the home buyer. However, as prices continue
to fall steeply, and as CAL cassettes and discs
become widely available, it is highly likely that
home-based educational software using the
microcomputer will .... (increase/decrease) in
the years immediately ahead.

Type I or D

Frame 7.10

Knowing that most metals expand when heated, and remembering that the period of a pendulum depends on the length of the rod, we would expect that a pendulum clock would .... (gain/lose) time on a cold day.

Frame 7.11

Wine is made from grapes grown and fermented in the district of its origin and is not fortified. Sherry consists of fine red wine fortified with brandy.

Is sherry a wine?

Type Y or N

Frame 7.12

A credit entry is made in the (left/right)-hand side of the ledger.

Type L or R

Frame 7.13

In physics the three primary colours are red, blue and green. But an artist produces all his secondary colours from mixtures of red, blue and yellow.

Type T or F

Frame 7.14

The species of man is:
1. So advanced that he was specially created.
2. A product of evolution like every other species of animal.
3. Not an animal at all.

Type 1, 2 or 3

Frame 7.15

An hermaphrodite is:

1. Male
2. Female
3. Both male and female
4. Neither male nor female

Type 1, 2, 3 or 4

disparate, then the frame can become altogether too trivial. Frame 7.15 is an unusual version of a multiple-choice L-frame.

7.9 MATCHING FORMAT

This is a useful sort of L-frame (Frame 7.16).

For this type of format the programmer can devise a flashing cursor which then jumps down to the next row of dots when a response has been made.

A matching format frame can also be used as an FT-frame (Frame 7.17).

As this is one of the final frames in the Unit, Frame 7.17 is, in effect, an examination question. Instead of reinforcing the student after his responses, the programmer can arrange for a score to appear on the screen.

7.10 CRITERION FORMAT

Criterion formats are simple question–type frames which are chiefly used as T or L-frames. Frames 7.18 and 7.19 are two examples.

Frame 7.19 is an example of an I-frame in which *two* new facts are being introduced simultaneously. This is extremely unusual and should only be done sparingly when it is likely, from the context, that both facts can be absorbed at once. Testing will reveal whether the supposition is correct.

7.11 SHORT-ANSWER FORMAT

Frames 7.20 and 7.21 are taken from a GCE O-level Physics Unit.

In Frame 7.21 the student will have to do some calculations. He might do this on a separate piece of paper and then type his answer onto the keyboard. However, the microcomputer lends itself admirably to doing calculations and can be programmed to go into calculation mode. This is done in the following sort of format.

7.12 EXERGUE FORMAT

This is a format which is commonly used in Mathematics and Physics Units (Frame 7.22).

The program is coded so that the microcomputer identifies the answer from the rest of the calculations by the underlining.

7.13 MNEMONIC FORMAT

Some examples of mnemonics have already been given. Frame 7.23 is another one from an O-level Biology Unit.

Once again, the CAL writer should not shrink from using mnemonics.

Frame 7.16

Match each item on the left with its correct unit on the right by typing its number in the corresponding space. The first has been done for you.

1. Acceleration   ..... m/s
2. Deceleration   ..... s
3. Velocity $(-)$ ..... m/s^2
4. Distance $(+)$ ⊡ m/s^2
5. Time   ..... m

Type READY after each response

Frame 7.17

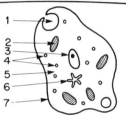

Animal cell

... nuclear membrane ... centriole
... contractile vacuole ... cytoplasm
... fat globules ... mitochondrion
... ectoplasm

Frame 7.18

The energy depots in an animal cell consist of .... droplets and .... granules.

Frame 7.19

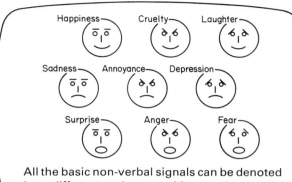

All the basic non-verbal signals can be denoted by ... different eyebrow positions and ... mouth shapes.

Frame 7.20

Write the usual formula connecting u, v, a and t

Frame 7.21

A tennis ball is thrown vertically upwards and it immediately decelerates until it stops for a moment before falling. If it is thrown at 60 m/s, and its deceleration is -10 m/s^2, calculate how long it will take to reach its maximum height.

Frame 7.22

A tennis ball is thrown vertically upwards and it immediately decelerates until it stops for a moment before falling. If it is thrown at 60 m/s, and its deceleration is -10 m/s^2 calculate how long it will take to reach its maximum height.

FOR YOUR CALCULATIONS

UNDERLINE YOUR ANSWER

Frame 7.23

All living organisms have the following characteristics:

Movement, Assimilation, Respiration, Reproduction, Irritability, (And), Growth, Excretion.

To help you remember these characteristics you can use a Memory Word consisting of the initial letters of the above.

This word is ....

Frame 7.24

After food substances have been absorbed by the living cell, they are digested and then asimilated by the organs in the cell.

CORRECT

Unfortunately, your response was mis-spelled. It should have had two 's's. Type this again correctly

....

Indeed, half an hour spent on composing a striking and memorable one is well worth while. A mnemonic is at its best when it is used to remember a cluster of terms not normally found together but often asked for in examination questions. It is bad practice, however, for the CAL writer to teach a mnemonic for a concept or formula in order to avoid teaching important preliminary stages.

7.14 INCORRECT RESPONSES

Sometimes a CAL writer will allow for trial and error learning by writing frames in which incorrect responses are as likely as correct ones. These are called *experiential formats* and are discussed in the next section. In this section we confine ourselves to frames from which the writer expects a correct response, but gets an incorrect one.

Now in the vast majority of cases, frames which elicit more than 2 or 3% of incorrect responses during field testing are totally rewritten, and then tested again to ensure that they are answered correctly.

But there are some situations where a writer might feel that it will do no great harm to allow for a proportion of mistakes. He therefore asks the programmer to build in a small branching routine. We don't normally recommend remedial branches because it encourages sloppy program writing, but for some popularly mis-spelled words, for example, it is acceptable. In Frame 7.24 the required response is 'assimilated'. The programmer allows for one common mistake, namely 'asimilate' as shown.

The branch could then contain a further T-frame to ensure that the spelling has been done correctly before returning to the main program.

However, *all* other mis-spellings of 'assimilate' cannot be anticipated by the writer nor programmed into the microcomputer. Even if there were enough memory space in the micro it would be a waste of programming. Usually, it is best to 'fix' possible mis-spellings before they occur, but in cases like the above it does no harm. Decisions on these sorts of branches should be considered after the field testing, not before.

7.15 EXPERIENTIAL FORMAT

We have already discussed the fact that, sometimes, incorrect responses are not allowed for, but positively welcomed by the CAL writer. In these cases, the student will be just as reinforced whether his response was correct or not. Frame 7.25 is an example. It follows a series of frames in which the student has learned to discriminate (in some straightforward cases) between fruits and vegetables.

Most students (most readers, possibly!) will reply incorrectly to this question. If the student correctly answers 'No' then the program moves on to

Frame 7.25

Is the pineapple a fruit?

Type Y or N

Frame 7.26

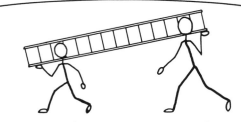

Who is carrying more weight?

1. The father.
2. The son.
3. Both of them, equally.

Type 1, 2 or 3

Frame 7.27

If all the people of the world were able to stand on one another's shoulders would they reach the moon?

Type Y or N

Frame 7.28

Type up to 50 words on how government subsidies to a domestic industry are used to restrict the import of similar goods from abroad.

UNDERLINE THE LAST WORD IN YOUR PASSAGE

Frame 7.29

Subsidies allow a domestic industry to sell its goods more cheaply. This means that customers will buy these goods rather than imported ones. Thus the demand for the foreign goods will be *reduced*.

Frame 7.30

Subsidies allow a domestic industry to sell its goods more cheaply. This means that customers will buy these goods rather than imported ones. Thus the demand for the foreign goods will be *reduced*.

Your answers should include the following points:
1. Home produced goods can be produced and sold more CHEAPLY.
2. Home produced goods therefore become more COMPETITIVE.
3. Therefore, consumers will buy MORE home produced goods.
4. Therefore, FEWER foreign goods will be bought.

Did you make all these points?

the next frame. If he replies 'Yes' then a remedial frame can be shown explaining why the pineapple is not a fruit.

Frame 7.26 is another experiential frame from the beginning of a Unit on mechanics.

Frame 7.27 is a rather silly I-frame from the Population Unit of an O-level Geography course. It gets a good point across, though!

7.16 FREE-RANGE FORMAT

In all the frame formats shown so far in this chapter the programmer will be able to instruct the microcomputer to know exactly what to do according to the responses of the student. But, in Units which are designed to reach examination question objectives there will be a need to ask those sorts of questions towards the end of the Unit. Some of these questions will consist of labelled drawings, or of descriptive passages, etc. None of these sorts of responses can be assessed by the microcomputer. Frame 7.28 is an example; it is an FT-frame from a GCE O-level Economics Unit on international trade.

Let us imagine that a student replies as in Frame 7.29.

Immediately – *whatever* the student's response – the microcomputer replies with Frame 7.30.

There is, of course, no way at present that a microcomputer can be programmed to understand and evaluate such a complex statement. The so-called 'fifth generation' computers, on which huge sums of money are now being spent, might be able to do this in many years to come.

7.17 CHECK LIST

There is no reason why you should not discover other formats in the course of your CAL writing. Also, as home and educational microcomputers continue to be developed, other formats will become possible. For the time being, however, to help you to consider a variety of formats you can use the check list in Table 7.1 if you wish. Remember, though, that the format is chosen *last*. After deciding on the structure of your Unit, you then decide on the distribution of frame types. Then, and only then, should you consider what formats to use.

7.18 EXAMPLES OF POOR FRAME WRITING

Here we show examples of frames that leave something to be desired. One of the most frequent mistakes made by new CAL writers is in calling for an inappropriate response. The original intention may have been well conceived and the frame began to write itself in what the writer felt was a satisfying way. Somehow, an invisible 'twist' occurred in the frame (Frame 7.31).

Table 7.1

Alternative appropriate frame formats	Frame types			
	I	T	L	FT
No-response	–	–	–	–
Copy	★	–	–	–
Cued	★	★	–	–
Criterion	★	★	★	–
Faded prompt	–	★	★	–
Two-choice	–	★	★	–
Multiple-choice	–	★	★	–
Experiential	–	★	★	–
Matching	–	★	★	★
Mnemonic	–	★	★	★
Short answer	–	–	★	★
Exergue	–	–	★	★
Free range	–	–	–	★

The obvious point of Frame 7.31 is to elicit the *contraction* of petrol when cooled, not that petrol is a liquid. The second sentence of this frame should therefore read:

'Petrol is a liquid and will . . . . in cold weather.'

Frame 7.32 suffers from several faults which can best be summarized as 'textbookitis'.

This would be a normal sort of paragraph in a text book. As a teaching frame in a CAL Unit it is totally unacceptable. Firstly, it has a rather superior, lecturing tone: '(We) Physicists . . . .'. The CAL writer is not a superior person handing down some precious substance called knowledge to the learner, but a partner in the learning process. CAL writers, and other instructional authors, who are writing for non-examinable students normally don't go in for pedantic discriminations. But these litter examination questions and disfigure many a text book. No doubt all these discriminations are important later rather than sooner, but text-book writers are often all too eager to fetch them up right at the beginning of a topic and either confuse or bore the student. Leave such discriminations until as late as possible in the Unit or the course of study. If, however, you can't avoid them – because they are bound to appear in an examination question – then adopt a friendly relationship with the learner by saying something like: 'Look, this *is* rather tedious, but it will give you a couple of marks in the examination . . .'.

A second major fault with Frame 7.32 is that the response could easily be

Frame 7.31

Generally speaking, gases, liquids and solids will contract when cooled. Petrol is a .... and will contract in cold weather.

Frame 7.32

The average speed of a vehicle travelling 120 <u>km</u> in 2 <u>h</u> is 60 <u>km/h</u>. The formula is:

$$\text{average speed} = \frac{\text{distance}}{\text{time}}$$

Physicists, however, differentiate between speed and velocity, even though their units are just the same. Velocity is concerned with 'displacement' and this means 'distance travelled in a definite direction'. So a velocity has direction as well as magnitude (size) whereas speed has only magnitude.

Therefore,

$$\text{average velocity} = \frac{\text{d}..........}{\text{time}}$$

Frame 7.33

You have already learned that velocity is concerned with displacement, not distance.

Therefore, the formula for average velocity is:

$$\frac{\text{d}..........}{\text{time}}$$

answered without any thought at all, by simply noting the symmetry between the two formulae. The third major fault is that the frame is congested with too much new material. This frame needs to be rewritten into at least half a dozen new frames.

One criticism that has not been made about the previous frame is that it was too wordy. Lengthy frames *per se* are not necessarily a bad thing. Indeed, long frames, if written well with short sentences and a simple, direct style, can often be read quicker than shorter frames. Moreover, long frames every now and again add variety to a Unit and also keep the student in touch with the real world when longer spans of attention are often required. A long frame is often useful in order to bury a cue to the correct response, to ensure that the student reads the whole passage. This is particularly useful when fairly sophisticated concepts are being taught. The cue, however, should always be fair and never obscure.

Sometimes, the CAL writer may want to give the student the chance of pausing by giving him a diversion. In a long frame you can enrich the material with metaphors, analogies and even short anecdotes. Such a frame need not always elicit a response, but if it does so then the CAL writer must be quite sure what specific point is being made; it should never become a shaggy dog story.

Extremely easy responses are allowable in I-frames in order to give a gentle introduction to a new concept or a difficult spelling, but they are not desirable in L-frames or T-frames (Frame 7.33).

In Frame 7.33, the word 'displacement' has already been introduced in an earlier I-frame. L-frames such as Frame 7.33 must always seek to reduce the amount of prompting once a new term has been introduced. This frame, therefore, is overcued; there is no need to have the 'd' as a prompt.

The rule with cues and prompts is that, once a new fact is introduced, they should be progressively withdrawn. There is just one special circumstance when the CAL writer may have to consider *re*prompting. Let us assume that a Unit is a lengthy one and that a cluster of new material is taught at the beginning of the Unit; then, for intrinsic reasons the Unit has to change its style or content for a period while a new concept is being considered. The writer might then wish to combine elements of the former with the latter. In this case, the early material, well learned by the student in its earlier context might need slight reprompting in order to bring it to life again in the new circumstances. The need for this can only be gauged during pilot trials.

Frame 7.34 is an example of an enriched frame. The biographical details of the inventor are not called for in the syllabus but they add more interest to the Unit. The writer has gone awry for another reason.

An assumption has been made that the learner would recognize the relationship between 100 degrees, boiling water and the *centigrade* scale of temperature. Some students would be quite capable of writing 'Fahrenheit' as the response. It would be better taught in two stages:

Frame 7.34

Anders Celsius, an astronomer, invented the centigrade scale of temperature. A thermometer which reads 100 degrees in boiling water is measuring the temperature of the water according to the .... scale of temperature.

Frame 7.35

The centigrade scale of temperature can also be called the .... scale after the name of its inventor.

Frame 7.36

Anders Celsius, an astronomer, invented the centigrade scale of temperature. For this reason a centigrade thermometer is often called a .... thermometer.

(a) The relationship between *100* and *centi*grade, and
(b) The relationship between 100 degrees and the (constant) temperature of boiling water.

Then the two separate parts can be drawn together. Mind you, it is debatable whether all this verbal palaver is necessary in this case. The relationships could be taught much more satisfactorily by graphics methods.

Let us assume that Frame 7.34 was sorted out. Immediately afterwards occurs another faulty frame (Frame 7.35).

This is well phrased but unfair because the writer is assuming that the student would have remembered the name of Celsius from the previous frame. This is most unlikely, easy though the fact was. It should have been taught as a specific I-frame as shown in Frame 7.36.

Frame 7.36 is a legitimate teaching frame which elicits the name of the inventor. Also, the student is stretched just a little more by the subtle change from using 'scale of temperature' to 'thermometer'. To ensure that the name of Celsius has been well and truly learned it must be associated with centigrade in further L-frames and tested a few times with progressively less prompting. Also, a separate series of L-frames should consolidate the connection between centigrade and 100 degrees.

The mention of graphics raises another matter which is frequently a fault in some programs. Never hesitate to use graphics and other sorts of visual help *if* you know exactly why you are doing it. It may be that it gets the point over more succinctly; it may be purely enrichment; it may be for the sake of variety in an otherwise tedious–looking Unit; and it may even be just a creative whim of the CAL writer. There is nothing wrong with any of these reasons *so long as* the writer knows what it is. However, some graphics can obscure the teaching point. A well-known example of this is a sequence of CAL frames frequently shown at exhibitions of educational technology. It is of an excavator with a movable arm and a shovel that can scoop and then deposit its load. The learner has huge fun in operating the excavator and loading a pile of soil onto a lorry. It is a superb piece of graphics and it is very popular with visitors. It is, however, an *inappropriate* series of frames because, while all the loading and shovelling is going on, a very important teaching point about robotics is being put across *but not absorbed*. If you ask users what they have learned, they reply: 'how to load a lorry with an excavator.'! Now there is no reason why the CAL writer, the program coder and the learner should not all have some fun with a few frames such as this. However, the teaching point must be got across clearly as soon as the fun is finished.

We end with two frames that were symptomatic of a major error made by the CAL writer. In the end they caused him to restructure over 100 frames in the Unit. The frames were as shown in Frames 7.37 and 7.38.

Intrinsically, these frames were well written. It was not until testing was

Frame 7.37

A great many things in life are in a state of *balance*. During the day the earth gets warmer because the sunlight heats it up. But at night the earth cools down.

From month to month and year to year the earth's temperature stays the same. This means that heat received from the sun during the day is exactly .... by heat given off during the night.

Frame 7.38

A successful business is also in a state of balance. The money coming into the business (e.g. from sales) is exactly .... by the money leaving the business (e.g. cost of goods, rent, heating and lighting, etc.).

carried out that the writer began to realize that the concept of 'balance' (in bookkeeping terms) was not being understood. He then realized that 'balance' was not being sufficiently linked with other facts being taught in the Unit. More L-frames were added. But 'balance' was still not understood by the time the students had reached the FT-frames. The writer then realized that 'balance', an apparently simple term was, in fact, too advanced to be used in an early Unit. The concept was then stripped out of the Unit altogether and the whole Unit was reconstructed. The concept of 'balance' did not occur again until three Units later, after which time the student had completed many examples of Trial Balances and hardly needed to be taught the concept separately. This is yet another example of the wisdom of starting with vague concepts and definitions and then shaping them up later.

8
Preparation, writing and testing

You are now at the stage where you are facing the most dreadful thing known to man – the piece of white paper before you. How to start! We have still got a few points to discuss yet, but it will be convenient now to lay out the stages through which a CAL Unit will pass:

1. Task analysis and establishing the educational objectives of the Unit.
2. Deciding upon the Unit structure and the frame type distribution.
3. Validation by a subject matter expert.
4. Pilot trial, followed by modifications to 1 and 2 above if necessary.
5. Field testing, following by modifications if necessary.
6. Coding by assembly programmer.
7. Documentation and publication.

The last stage will be discussed in the following chapter. We will now go through the other stages systematically, discussing new points and recapitulating briefly on those we have already covered in the course of the book.

8.1 TASK ANALYSIS

This is probably the most daunting of all the tasks facing the CAL writer. There is only one way, and this is to saturate yourself in the subject you are going to teach. So long as you have the intellectual ability, it will not matter if you are not initially acquainted with it. Indeed, it has advantages because you will experience many of the problems that face the student. On no account simply open a text book at page 1 and start writing frames for your first Unit. You will find, appearances to the contrary, that the conceptual and teaching content of a text book varies considerably from chapter to chapter and from section to section. You will frequently find that the final 'product mix' of your Units will differ considerably from the relative numbers of pages given in a text book to different parts of the subject. The more that you study several different text books in a particular subject the more you will find that it starts to take shape in the form of a conceptual hierarchy – if you like, an organization chart.

After saturating yourself in a subject you will meet one, and possibly two, dilemmas. The first one is the dawning realization that you will never be able to write CAL programs for more than a small part of the subject. Let us take an O-level subject as an example, such as Geography. A student could not possibly cover the syllabus in less than, say, 150 hours study. This will therefore require at least 150 CAL Units. Each CAL Unit, from start to finish, will take at least 200 hours of preparation (including the programmer's time). Some Units may take up to 300 or 400 hours preparation. This is totally different from text-book writing. Most O-level text books are quite able to be written by one author, and usually are. But text books do not teach the subject: they merely lay out the information. A typical O-level text book can be written in two or three years. However, if you do your arithmetic you will realize that you would only be able to write a very small fraction of this in the same period. It would take you, as a single writer, a whole lifetime to cover the same ground.

The second dilemma that might rear its head is that, after initial study, you will come to the conclusion that the subject matter lends itself to an approach quite different from those adopted by text-book writers. This is often the case when we are considering a subject in which the student will be facing an examination sooner or later. How you resolve this one will have to be left to you. However, this dilemma turns out to be not as great as it at first appears. As we have already discussed above, you will only be able to write small parts of an overall syllabus. You will find that, whether you start with a fresh overall strategy or whether you accept the examination-orientated strategies of the text-book writer, you will have atomized the subject into Unit-sized pieces anyway. From whichever direction you start you will end up with similar groupings of information at the Unit level of analysis.

This modular concept of CAL fits in very well with some extremely significant features about the skills and professions of tomorrow. As mentioned in Chapter 1, we are becoming an increasingly specialized society. But these specializations are not, as it were, detailed subdivisions of the existing conventional subject areas on which our present-day school, university and professional examinations are based. The new specializations will be cross-disciplinary. This is already a significant feature of modern science and modern industries and services. The jobs of tomorrow will consist of quite new permutations of skills and knowledge from different subject areas. There will, in fact, be such a proliferation and diversity of new professions that it is doubtful whether the existing examination-based educational system will be able to cope. The modularization of modern education, of which CAL will be a considerable feature, once again has radical consequences for the way in which educational publishing will develop. This is discussed further in the next chapter.

Returning to task analysis, there are some authorities who say that subject matters can be analysed in specific ways. For example, Bloom and others, authors of *Taxonomy of Educational Objectives* [18], consider that all learning tasks can be broken down into three specific components, namely cognitive (to do with thinking), affective (involving the emotions) and psycho-motor (physical activities). Another educationalist, Robert Gagné, in the latest edition of *The Conditions of Learning* [19] considers that educational tasks should be analysed in terms of five components: intellectual skills, cognitive strategies, verbal information, motor skills and attitudes. I have substantial reservations about both these approaches for the practising CAL writer. I find them impossibly difficult to carry out. The reason for this lies in the very nature of permanent memory in the neocortex. All long-term memories in the brain, whether they are of physical skills, cognitive skills, information and so on are all spread throughout the neocortex. This is one of the epochal discoveries of the brain made by Lashley over 30 years ago [20]. All skills, memories, abilities and so on are all inextricably intertwined within the whole of the neocortex. All networks involve emotion (from the hypothalamus) when they are laid down and all networks, even those consisting of the most abstract thoughts, involve physical manifestations, whether they are overt and observable or microscopic and not observable. We cannot classify learning tasks into watertight compartments because the brain does not do so.

As you analyse a subject into smaller and smaller constituents you will find many different sorts of learning tasks. Sometimes the task will be one of successively refining a general concept, sometimes you will be discriminating between different items of information, sometimes you will be simply presenting streams of facts to be learned. There is hardly any point in defining them or classifying them. The more you study the subject matter before you the clearer the individual tasks become. Therefore, an overall task analysis, let us say for O-level Geography, will break down into a hierarchy consisting of many different tasks, each of a slightly different character.

The best thing to do now is to look at some practical examples. Let us take O-level Biology. After perusing the relevant text books it does not take long to appreciate that the principal characteristic of the subject (or rather, the O-level examination syllabus) is the sheer number of new technical terms that the student has to learn. The syllabus covers about a dozen functional sections of about the same length and complexity. The course as a whole therefore has a rather flat, lateral structure (Fig. 8.1).

Looking at each box we find that none of them are conceptually complex. The main task of the student is to learn the technical terms in each area. This particularly applies to 'The cell'. If we therefore analyse this in more detail we find once again that it is a flat, lateral structure consisting of a string of terms to be learned (Fig. 8.2).

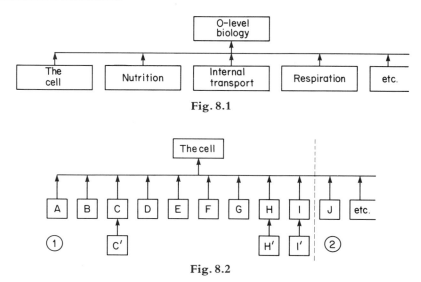

Fig. 8.1

Fig. 8.2

The dashed terms signify those which are given a little extra attention such as, for example, their Latin derivation, or the plural form of the term, etc. The circled numbers signify the first tentative breakdown that the CAL writer has made as to the terms he will teach in the Unit. The best convention to use is to proceed from the left-hand side towards the right, and also start from the bottom of a limb when it occurs.

Let us now look at O-level Economics. This time we find that there are about 15 to 20 functional areas of about the same length and complexity. So the initial analysis takes the same general form as in Fig. 8.1. Where economics differs greatly from biology, however, is that there are relatively few new technical terms to be learned. Even the technical terms have often been derived from ordinary language. The difficulty of task analysing economics is that many of the section headings contain some quite sophisticated relationships. For example, one of the main boxes could be 'Location of industry' and all sorts of qualitatively different factors might have to be connected, such as raw materials, accessibility of skilled manpower, transport routes, etc. One such box might therefore break down into something quite hierarchical (Fig. 8.3).

As you can see, the CAL writer has decided to group the teaching into two Units. In each case the letters give the order in which the information is handled.

O-level Mathematics is different again. We find that there are about a dozen functional areas but these are very variable in size. There are not many technical terms to learn but, on the other hand, there are some formidable conceptual manipulations to be done. The structure in Fig. 8.4 is the task analysis for one of the main sections.

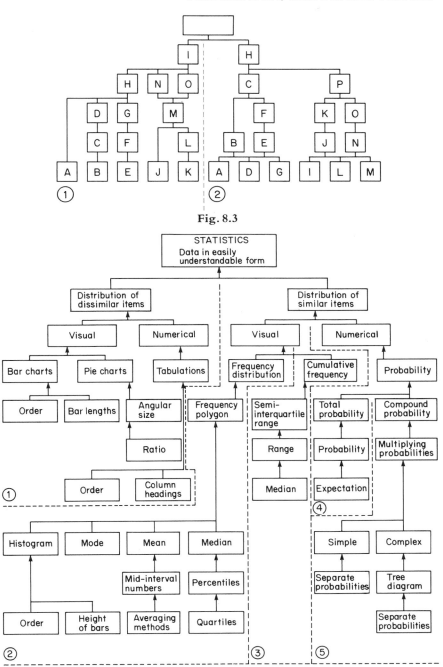

Fig. 8.3

Fig. 8.4

This turns out to be hierarchical and much less symmetrical than the economics one in Fig. 8.3. However, the shape of the above has been distorted in order to get it onto the page. You will notice that there are five Units in this part of the course. These five Units can be said to make up one *module*. As each Unit is part of an overall plan of the module it would not make sense for any of the Units to be purchased separately.

8.2 EDUCATIONAL OBJECTIVES

Each Unit should end with precise educational objectives. These are tasks that the student should be able to achieve after completing the Unit. They should be scorable so the CAL writer knows exactly how much has been learned. The educational objectives can also be used as pre-tests to ensure that the learner does not already know what the Unit will be covering.

If the Unit is teaching an examinable subject, and if the subject lends itself to a flat task analysis, such as O-level Biology, then it is possible that every Unit will end with actual examination questions. In some highly hierarchical subjects, like mathematics, the educational objectives will have to be questions of an intermediate level. Examination standard questions would have to be left until the end of a module of perhaps between two and 10 CAL Units.

An example of an educational objective is given in Appendix 1. This is an actual examination question. If, however, you have no specific examination question to guide you, then the following points will assist you:

1. *Conditions*: Are there any special circumstances involved? Will the student need apparatus, log tables, ordnance survey maps, etc.?
2. *Behaviour*: A precise description of what the student will actually do in meeting the objective. Avoid passive verbs like 'appreciate' and use active ones like 'choose', 'write', 'draw', 'label' and so on.
3. *Criterion*: The standard number of points that the student should achieve should be stated.

8.3 UNIT STRUCTURE AND FRAME TYPE DISTRIBUTION

This has already been discussed so there is no need to go into this any further. It is likely, though, that a clear idea of the structure of the Unit will be taking place in your mind during task analysis.

8.4 VALIDATION

If you are writing CAL programs in a subject that is new to you, it is obvious that you will need to vet your program – even at manuscript stage – with a subject matter expert. If substantial revisions follow later, then you might have to repeat the validation.

8.5 PILOT TRIAL

This is an extremely valuable stage in the preparation of a CAL Unit. Its importance can hardly be exaggerated. When you have completed a Unit to your satisfaction you will need a volunteer student who will try it at manuscript stage. A convenient way of doing this is to write each frame on a separate piece of A5 sized paper. The reinforcement is written at the top of the sheet but folded down so it is invisible to the student. As soon as the student writes his response at the bottom of the sheet, he is instructed to disclose the reinforcement *immediately*.

Sit with the student but say nothing by way of explanation as he works his way through the Unit. There will be some, perhaps many, frames that the student will be unable to respond to. He will, of course, ask you to explain. Do not do so. Write some additional or remedial frames on the spot and give them to him. (The student will soon get used to this odd behaviour!) You may have to do this several times for one particular sequence or another. If you give a verbal explanation you run the risk of invalidating a sequence of frames, so don't do so. Of course, you don't have to be a Trappist monk. When the student gets a correct response, you can smile or say 'Well Done!'. The final test-frames at the end of the Unit will show you exactly how effective your Unit has been.

There is another rule to be observed during the pilot trial. Whenever your pilot student cannot respond to a frame, or incorrectly responds to a frame for which you had anticipated a correct response, *never blame the student*. It will be your fault, not his. You will find this to be so in 99% of the cases. Your initial reaction will be one of annoyance that the student is being particularly obtuse, but this is very rarely so.

Another valuable part of the session is the *post mortem*. Discuss the Unit with the student when he has completed it. You will gain all sorts of insights from this. Even if he had got everything correct (which almost *never* happens!) he will still be able to tell you which sequences were interesting and which were boring, which sequences could do with more (or less) explanation.

The pilot trial can range from anything between being moderately successful, needing a few revisions, and disastrous, needing, sometimes, a completely new task analysis and rewrite. Don't regret having to do the latter if necessary. It is part of the training of a good CAL writer that money can't buy. If it's any consolation, this won't happen many times, but each time that you do have to do it your skill will be improving by leaps and bounds.

8.6 FIELD TESTING

After major or minor revisions following the pilot trail, and while your Unit is still in manuscript form, give it to several students of your target ability. Excluding experiential frames, what you need to know now is the success rate of the Unit both longitudinally and latitudinally. For each student you will need to reach a 95% success rate from the first frame in the Unit until the last. For each particular frame, and latitudinally across all the students, you will also need to reach something like a 95% success rate. The group of students who are helping you may not be large enough to make your results statistically valid in the strictest sense, but any poor frames will stick out like sore thumbs, particularly when you analyse your results latitudinally.

8.7 CODING

It is only at this stage that it is worth while getting your Unit coded. Microcomputers are improving so rapidly that you might as well find yourself a good programmer – someone who can program in assembly language. Make sure that you are always accessible to the programer in order to explain any ambiguities.

Also ensure that your programmer thoroughly documents the program. (This is not to be confused with *your* documentation, discussed in the next chapter.) The reason for program documentation is that if your Unit is a good one and acquires a good reputation there is no reason why it should not 'migrate' from one microcomputer to another many times and for many years. You will have invested a great deal of time and skill in the Unit and it will be nonsensical to confine it to one model of microcomputer with its inevitably short life. If your programmer has documented the program well, then further translations and enhancements will be relatively straightforward.

9
Publishing CAL

9.1 DOCUMENTATION

There is still a little more writing to be done! Your CAL tape or disc needs to be documented so that a potential purchaser knows exactly what he is buying. It should consist of the following sections:

1. General title, together with the name of the examination aimed for, if appropriate.
2. Publisher's reference number and more specific title of the Unit.
3. The duration of the Unit for the target student.
4. The microcomputer (together with RAM version and model number if relevant) for which the Unit has been programmed.
5. The educational objective of the Unit.

This is largely self–explanatory. A sample of Unit documentation is given in Appendix 1.

9.2 COPYRIGHT

At present there is no copyright law for computer software. There are very strong pressures for this already from large software houses and micro manufacturers. The reason why the courts have not yet ruled clearly in cases of plagiarism is that the legal profession is not yet happy with the idea that information can be encoded in electronic form. The courts are a little happier if programs are embodied in slightly more tangible form, such as a ROM chip, but even here there has been little case law. However, we may be sure that the pressure is so strong that copyright laws will be enacted soon. In the case of the UK it is likely to be EEC law.

Ideas cannot be protected, anyway. Under present copyright law you can take an idea from a novel or a play and make a film script using the same idea with impunity. Therefore, even under new software copyright, new ideas, however brilliant, can still be widely copied. Two outstanding examples, each with dozens of imitators, are Visicalc, in the commercial field, and PacMan, in the micro games field.

Whether under existing copyright law or in future software legislation, it would seem that educational software is safe. The reason for this is that it is the precise form in which the ideas are expressed, that is words on the screen, which is important.

Although ideas cannot be protected under present copyright law, the form in which these ideas are expressed can be. The form is usually words, of course. In educational software the precise form of words that appears on the screen is its most important feature. Even quite minor changes in the words of a frame will invalidate its purpose. It is probable that no-one will be able to change all the words of every frame, and the diagrams, and the formats, and still retain the integrity of the Unit. Although piracy in the world of educational software has not occurred yet, as far as is known, it is as well to take as many precautions as possible.

Here are some suggestions. At the manuscript stage, after field testing but *before* coding, lodge a sealed, dated copy of your Unit with your bank or solicitor. Another thing you could do instead – and this is done by some authors – post a copy to yourself and file the unopened envelope. It would be a good idea to read a little further about existing copyright [21]. At the present time, small educational software publishers are springing up like mushrooms. Generally speaking, unless you are sure about them, avoid them. Send your material only to large and reputable publishers. And don't sell your copyright.

9.3 CAL PUBLISHERS

Who are these CAL publishers likely to be? First and foremost at present are the existing book publishers, particularly those which have large educational departments. Books on microcomputing are about the only ones that are doing well in the UK and the United States at present, so it is not surprising that all major book publishers have started CAL departments in the last eighteen months or so. All of them will be eager to publish good CAL software in the form of discs and tapes. However, what the CAL writer must bear in mind is that CAL publishing, wide though it already is, will grow enormously in the coming years. Within a very short time indeed, CAL could be published in other forms, such as being downloaded from the telephone wire, cable or directly from satellite. Read Appendix 3 to get some idea about the fantastic rate of development in communications and informational technology. While book publishers are very happy at present to add discs and tapes to books, they may not make the conceptual leap required into electronic publishing from satellite. Companies that might seem to be unlikely candidates at present, such as Reuters International, the news agency, Haynes Television or Western Union, the biggest user of satellite communications in the United States, may, in fact, turn out to be the principal CAL publishers of tomorrow.

9.4 MULTI-PUBLISHING

One of the leading educational computing consultants in the United States, Shotwell and Associates, have already hinted that CAL publishing is likely to take the form of multi-publishing [22]. This is that any particularly good CAL Unit is likely to be published simultaneously by different publishers. This will be the means by which a good CAL writer will be able to earn at least as much as a text-book writer. The modular nature of CAL writing means that a Unit or a group of Units may find itself on several different publishers' lists as part of a variety of courses. For example, some frames from a module of two Units on international trade have been shown in this book. This module was originally writen for GCE O-level Economics in the UK, but the module could just as aptly appear in a business degree course in the United States or part of a preliminary course of accountancy in Australia. It could easily be translated into other languages and appear in many countries as parts of many different courses.

9.5 INTERACTIVE VIDEO

Interactive video is a system by which film, on video disc or video tape, is interlaced with CAL programs presented by a microcomputer. Not only can the two media be interlaced, but also they can be superimposed on the same screen. At the moment a great deal of interactive video is fairly crude and mainly consists of long film recordings interspersed with not very apt graphics produced by the microcomputer. As with 'straight' CAL, large resources are being poured into interactive video. This is likely to be even more expensive to produce than CAL. Besides paying royalties on existing film, or making new film, *two* lots of software have to be created, one for the micro and one for the video. However, if interactive video becomes effective as a teaching technology – as it no doubt will be – then it will still have to follow the inescapable laws of good teaching practice: analysis of material into small steps, opportunities for the student to actively work on those steps and, last but not least, reinforcement. It would therefore be very sensible for interactive video companies to pay royalties to writers of effective CAL software because they will have done the educational homework for them.

9.6 FUTURE SCENARIO

Making forecasts about the future is fraught with difficulties and what follows is as likely to be wrong as right. However, I will make a shot:

1983 onwards: Steady expansion of a wide variety of short, non-modular CAL programs (up to 48K) mainly for use in schools. Also, much CAL that can be used for demonstration purposes by teachers using networks of micros controlled from master unit with disc drives.

1984 onwards: Presentation of real-time CAL on public cable networks. Instant downloading of some CAL software via satellite/cable networks in America.

1985 onwards: Downloading of CAL suitable for 40-minute study sessions (256K chip will be widely available) from satellite transmissions via dish aerials into homes, schools and universities in Europe, North America and Japan.

1987 onwards: Downloading of CAL up to 1024K length, and massive expansion of educational courses available in modular CAL form. Beginnings of expansion of educational channels on national satellites in even the poorest countries. (£1000 will probably buy all the equipment that a village will need for its school in order to become the educational equivalent of several universities.)

1990 onwards: Downloading of extensive CAL/interactive video Units into Western homes able to afford large memory chips. Consequent rapid expansion of training in, and proliferation of, new informational professions.

All the above is already technically possible and most of it seems economically viable. The only likely constraint will be the likely shortage of CAL software.

Let us end with two final quotations. The first is from the Shotwell and Associates' Report already mentioned:

> The potential is enormous; it (CAL) could tap into a very high percentage of the entire installed base of microcomputers . . . Home delivery of education could rapidly become the primary *modus operandi.* [22]

The second is from a recent market survey carried out by Strategic Incorporated:

> Home use of educational software is outstripping its introduction into schools. [23]

Goodbye and best wishes for your CAL software!

Appendix 1

An exemplary CAL Unit (Biology)

The Unit shown in this appendix is the second in an O-level Biology course. There are three parts:

- (i) Documentation.
- (ii) Frame record of writer.
- (iii) Unit 2 (Biology).*

(i) DOCUMENTATION

1. *BIOLOGY (O-LEVEL GCE).*
2. *BIOL-OL-2 Introduction to the cell.*
3. *Duration:* 50 minutes for average student.
4. *BBC microcomputer model B (32K) Tape version.*
5. *Educational objective.*

At the end of the Unit the student will be able to score at least 90% of possible marks from the following typical O-level question:

> Draw and label a typical plant cell and an animal cell showing ten main features in each case.
> Write a short passage describing five important differences between plant and animal cells.

(ii) FRAME RECORD OF WRITER

Figure A1.1 (which is displayed on pages 121–124) is the frame record that the CAL writer keeps *as he is writing* the Unit. The first two rows are self-explanatory. The third and fourth rows signify whether a response has been called for and a reinforcement given. Note that no–reinforcement frames are intermittent but become quite common towards the end of the Unit.

The rows under *Skill/fact/concept* keep a record of what has been introduced

---

* The specimen Unit that follows contains the frames that will appear on the screen. The reinforcements are not shown.

in that frame. By reading across the row as the Unit grows, an accurate record can be kept of the number of times the fact or concept is retested or linked. The name of the row is really only a shorthand version. Many concepts, comparisons, discriminations and enrichment material are not explicitly mentioned.

Frame number	1	2	3	4	5	6	7	8	9	10	11	12	13	14	15	16	17	18	19	20	21	22	23	24	25
Frame type	I	I	T	I	T	I	T	L	L	I	T	T	L	T	L	I	L	L	I	T	L	I	T	L	L
Response?	✓	✓	✓	✓	✓	✓	✓	✓	✓	✓	✓	✓	✓	✓	✓	✓	✓	✓	✓	✓	✓	✓	✓	✓	✓
Reinforcement?	✓	✓	✓	✓	✓	✓	✓	✓	✓	✓	✓	✓	✓	✓	■	✓	✓	✓	✓	✓	✓	✓	✓	✓	✓
Skill / fact / concept																									
drawing		1	2					3																	
rigid				1	2			3	4				5			6									
flexible						1	2	3	4			5	6			7		8							
cellulose											1	2		3	4						5				
membrane																1	2	3			4				
cytoplasm																			1	2	3			4	5
endoplasm																						1	2	3	4
ectoplasm																									
vacuole																									
contractile vacuole																									
permanent vacuole																									
nucleus																									
nucleolus																									
centriole																									
chloroplast																									
chlorophyll																									
mitochondria																									
starch grains																									
fat globules																									

Fig. A1.1 Frame record (Unit 2)

Frame number	26	27	28	29	30	31	32	33	34	35	36	37	38	39	40	41	42	43	44	45	46	47	48	49	50
Frame type	I	T	L	L	L	I	L	L	L	I	L	I	L	L	L	L	I	I	I	T	T	T	I	L	L
Response?	√	√	√	√	√	√	√	√	√	√	√	√	√	√	√	■	√	√	√	√	√	√	√	√	√
Reinforcement?	√	√	√	√	√	√	√	√	√	√	√	√	√	√	√	√	■	√	√	√	√	√	√	√	√
Skill/fact/concept																									
drawing																									
rigid								7							8										
flexible								9							10										
cellulose				6																					
membrane					5																				6
cytoplasm				6				7					8								9				
endoplasm			5	6									7				8								
ectoplasm	1	2	3	4	5								6				7								
vacuole						1	2	3	4		5		6		7		8				9				
contractile vacuole									1	2		3		4	5		6			7					
permanent vacuole											1	2		3			4			5					
nucleus																		1	2	3	4			5	6
nucleolus																						1		2	3
centriole																									
chloroplast																									
chlorophyll																									
mitochondria																									
starch grains																									
fat globules																									

Fig. A1.1 Frame record (Unit 2) (continued)

Frame number	51	52	53	54	55	56	57	58	59	60	61	62	63	64	65	66	67	68	69	70	71	72	73	74	75
Frame type	T	T	T	T	T	T	I	T	L	L	L	I	I	L	L	L	L	L	L	I	T	L	L	L	T
Response ?	✓	✓	✓	✓	✓	✓	✓	✓	✓	✓	✓	✓	✓	✓	✓	✓	✓	✓	✓	✓	✓	✓	✓	✓	✓
Reinforcement ?	✓	■	✓	■	✓	✓	✓	✓	✓	✓	■	✓	✓	✓	✓	✓	■	✓	✓	■	✓	✓	✓	✓	■
Skill / fact / concept																									
drawing																									
rigid				9							10														
flexible				11							12														
cellulose				7														8							
membrane	7				8													9							
cytoplasm		10																	11						
endoplasm		9																	10						
ectoplasm		8				9													10						
vacuole			10			11												12							13
contractile vacuole			8			9					10														
permanent vacuole			6								7							8							
nucleus				7				8																	
nucleolus			4		5			6	7							8				9					10
centriole							1	2	3	4	5				6					7			8		
chloroplast												1	2	3	4		5		6					7	
chlorophyll												1	2		3	4									
mitochondria																					1	2	3	4	5
starch grains																									
fat globules																									

Fig. A1.1 Frame record (Unit 2) (continued)

Frame number	76	77	78	79	80	81	82	83	84	85	86	87	88	89	90	91	92	93	94	95	96	97	98	99
Frame type	I	L	I	T	T	L	L	L	L	L	L	L	L	T	L	L	L	FT	T	FT	FT	T	FT	
Response?	✓	✓	✓	✓	✓	✓	✓	✓	✓	✓	✓	✓	✓	✓	✓	✓	✓	✓	✓	✓	✓	✓	✓	
Reinforcement?	✓	✓	✓	✓	■	■	✓	✓	■	✓	■	✓	■	✓	■	✓	✓	■	■	✓	■	■	✓	■
Skill/fact/concept																								
drawing									4		5												6	
rigid							11		12												13		14	
flexible								13			14	15									14		15	
cellulose								9													10		11	
membrane									10	11	12												13	
cytoplasm									12								13	14					15	
endoplasm											11						12	13					14	
ectoplasm											11										12		13	
vacuole									14	15		16	17										18	
contractile vacuole											11	12	13										14	
permanent vacuole									9	10			11										12	
nucleus									9			10											11	
nucleolus									11					12									13	
centriole										9	10	11									12		13	
chloroplast					8					9	10				11								12	
chlorophyll					5					6					7								8	
mitochondria		6							7		8	9								10			11	
starch grains	1	2		3		4			5	6	7								8			9	10	
fat globules			1	2	3		4					5							6			7	8	

Fig. A1.1 Frame record (Unit 2) (continued)

(iii) UNIT TWO BIOLOGY

Frame A1.1

In previous Units you will have learned that
plants and animals are composed of various
sorts of tissues such as stem, leaf, muscle, nerve,
etc.

In order to see what tissues are composed of we
have to look at very thin slices under a
microscope. You learned that all tissues are
composed of very small units. These are like
small, complicated chemical factories and are
called ....

Frame A1.2

One popular examination question is to draw
and label plant cells and animal cells. In the left-
hand area below draw a firm rectangle and label
it a plant cell. In the right-hand area draw a wavy
sort of oval and label this as an animal cell.

Frame A1.3

Draw a plant cell and an animal cell. Don't forget
to label them.

Frame A1.4

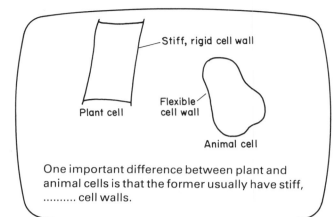

One important difference between plant and animal cells is that the former usually have stiff, ... cell walls.

Frame A1.5

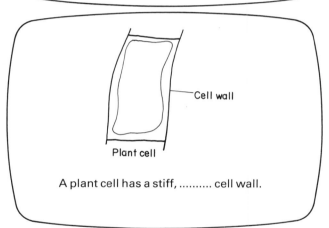

A plant cell has a stiff, ... cell wall.

Frame A1.6

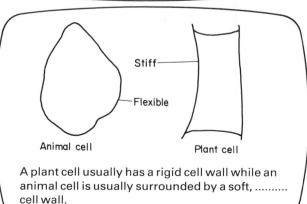

A plant cell usually has a rigid cell wall while an animal cell is usually surrounded by a soft, ... cell wall.

Frame A1.7

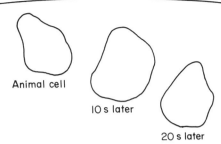

Animal cell

10 s later

20 s later

An animal cell can often change its shape quite quickly because it has a soft, pliable, ... cell wall.

Frame A1.8

Draw a plant cell and an animal cell and label them.

Then write labels showing what sort of cell walls they have.

Frame A1.9

A plant cell is .... because it normally doesn't change its shape.

On the other hand, an animal cell can often change its shape readily because it has soft, pliable, ... cell walls.

Frame A1.10

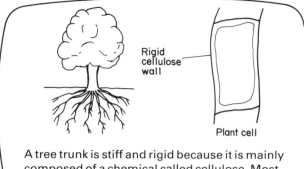

A tree trunk is stiff and rigid because it is mainly composed of a chemical called cellulose. Most plant cells are rigid because they have cell walls consisting of layers of ....

Frame A1.11

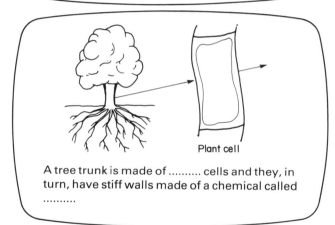

A tree trunk is made of .... cells and they, in turn, have stiff walls made of a chemical called ....

Frame A1.12

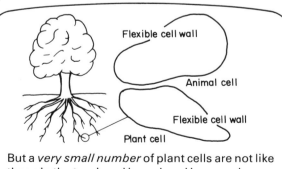

But a *very small number* of plant cells are not like those in the trunk and branches. Here we show a plant cell with a .... wall that is found at the growing tip of a tree ....

Frame A1.13

Plant cell

Plant cell

99.99% of plant cells have .... made of ....
but a very small number of plant cells in the tips
of the roots have to squeeze into cracks in the soil
and therefore have .... walls.

Frame A1.14

You now know that all animal cells and a very
small minority of plant cells are soft and flexible
because their cell walls are *not* composed of the
chemical called ....

Frame A1.15

One popular question in Biology examinations is
to ask what important differences there are
between animal and plant cells. You now know
that one difference is that most plant cells have

....

....

(COMPLETE THE SENTENCE IN YOUR OWN
WORDS. USE AT LEAST FIVE WORDS)

Frame A1.16

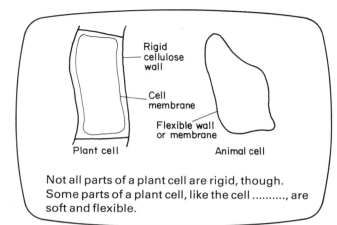

Not all parts of a plant cell are rigid, though. Some parts of a plant cell, like the cell ...., are soft and flexible.

Frame A1.17

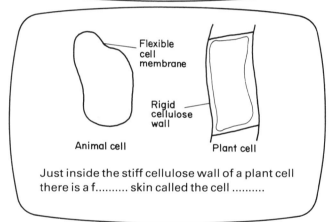

Just inside the stiff cellulose wall of a plant cell there is a f.......... skin called the cell ....

Frame A1.18

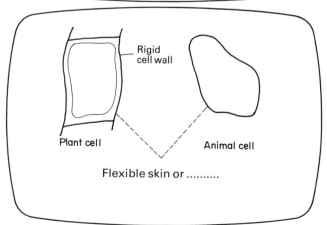

Frame A1.19

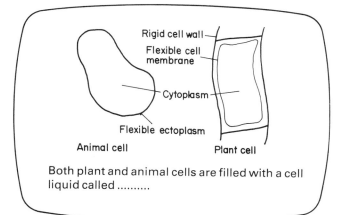

Both plant and animal cells are filled with a cell liquid called ....

Frame A1.20

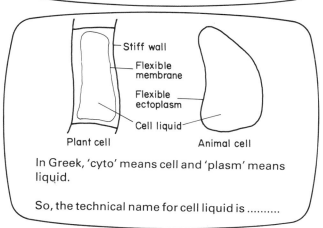

In Greek, 'cyto' means cell and 'plasm' means liquid.

So, the technical name for cell liquid is ....

Frame A1.21

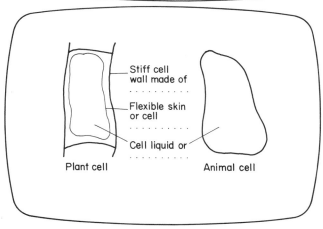

Frame A1.22

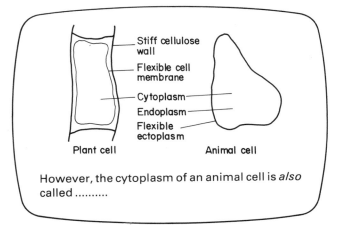

Plant cell   Animal cell

However, the cytoplasm of an animal cell is *also* called ....

Frame A1.23

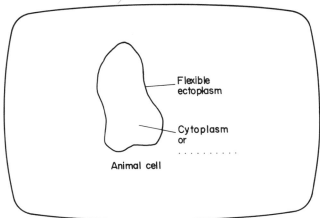

Animal cell

Frame A1.24

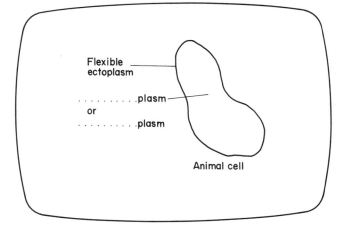

Animal cell

Frame A1.25

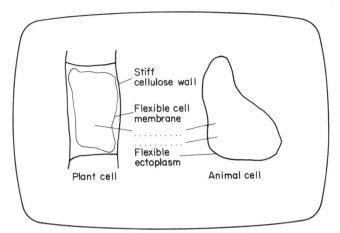

Frame A1.26

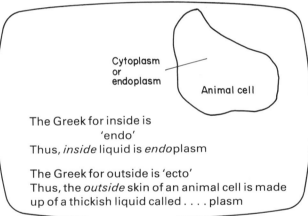

Frame A1.27

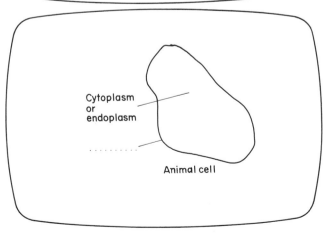

Frame A1.28

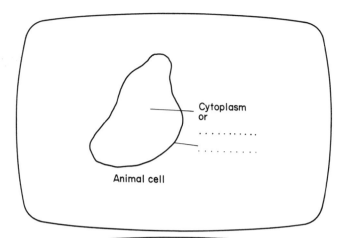

Frame A1.29

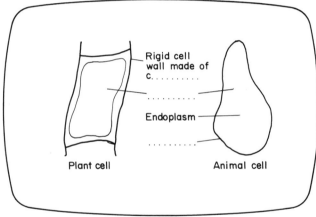

Frame A1.30

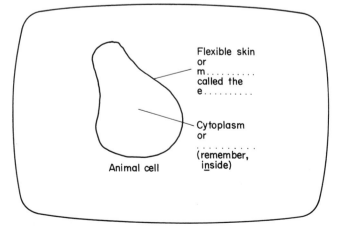

Frame A1.31

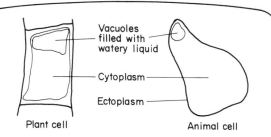

Vacuoles filled with watery liquid

Cytoplasm

Ectoplasm

Plant cell   Animal cell

Both plant and animal cells are filled with a 'soup' of cell liquid or cytoplasm. If these cytoplasms become too watery then the excess water collects in special 'bubbles' or ....

Frame A1.32

If a cytoplasm of a cell becomes too watery, then the excess .... moves to bubbles called ....

Frame A1.33

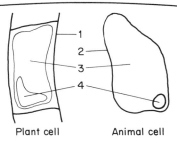

1
2
3
4

Plant cell   Animal cell

1. A .... cell wall consisting of cellulose
2. A .... cell wall called the ectoplasm
3. Cell fluid called ....
4. Watery bubbles called ....

Frame A1.34

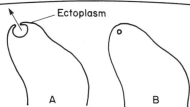

When a dam becomes dangerously full of water, engineers open sluice gates, which lets some of it away. When an animal cell becomes too watery, an opening appears in the ectoplasm and the excess water is squirted out as shown in A. When most of this has gone, the .... contracts to a very small bubble as in B.

Frame A1.35

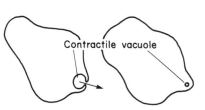

The vacuole in an animal cell is called a *contracti*le vacuole because it is constantly accumulating water and getting larger, and then suddenly expels the water by ....ing to a very small size.

Frame A1.36

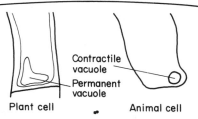

The vacuole in a plant cell doesn't change in size very much, so it is called a permanent vacuole. In contrast, the vacuole in an animal cell is enlarging and then suddenly contracting continually. For this reason it is called a .... vacuole.

Frame A1.37

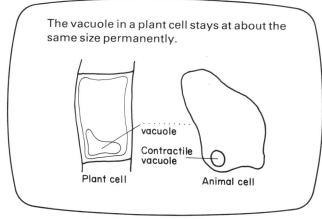

The vacuole in a plant cell stays at about the same size permanently.

vacuole

Contractile vacuole

Plant cell   Animal cell

Frame A1.38

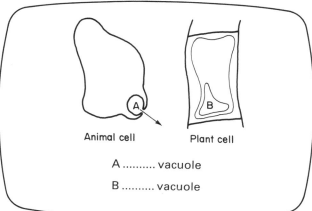

Animal cell   Plant cell

A .... vacuole

B .... vacuole

Frame A1.39

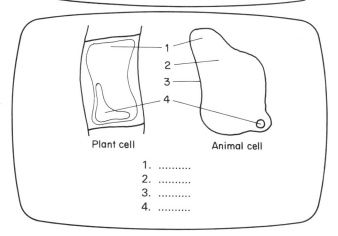

Plant cell   Animal cell

1. ....
2. ....
3. ....
4. ....

Frame A1.40

> Plant cells have large .... vacuoles. Animal cells have .... vacuoles.

Frame A1.41

> You have now learned *two* important differences between animal and plant cells.
>
> The first difference is that plant cells have a .... cell wall made of cellulose; but animal cell walls, or ectoplasms, are ....
>
> The second difference is that plant cells have permanent ...., but those of animal cells change size constantly because they slowly fill with excess water and then suddenly expel it through a hole in the ectoplasm. These are called .... vacuoles.

Frame A1.42

> Well done! Have a rest for a minute or two. You have now learned half of the new facts and ideas in this Unit.
>
> When you're ready, press RETURN and we'll be on our way again.

Frame A1.43

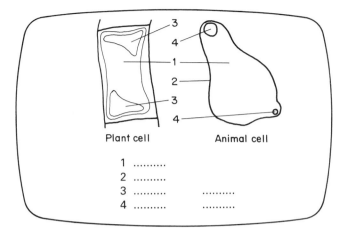

Plant cell   Animal cell

1 ....
2 ....
3 ....
4 ....

Frame A1.44

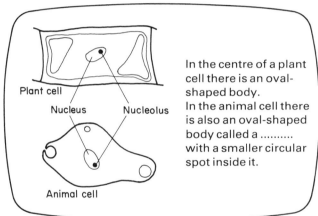

Plant cell

Nucleus   Nucleolus

Animal cell

In the centre of a plant cell there is an oval-shaped body.
In the animal cell there is also an oval-shaped body called a ....
with a smaller circular spot inside it.

Frame A1.45

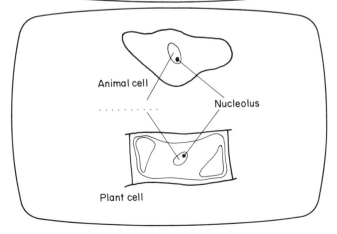

Animal cell

. . . .   Nucleolus

Plant cell

Frame A1.46

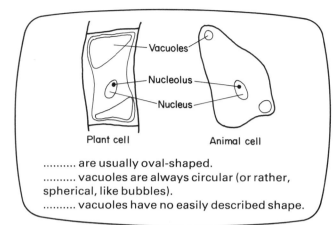

.... are usually oval-shaped.
.... vacuoles are always circular (or rather, spherical, like bubbles).
.... vacuoles have no easily described shape.

Frame A1.47

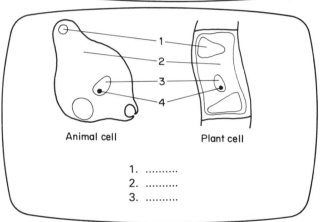

1. ....
2. ....
3. ....

Frame A1.48

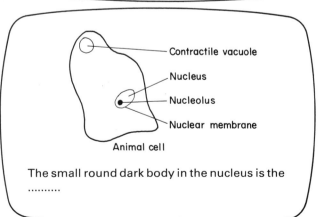

The small round dark body in the nucleus is the ....

Frame A1.49

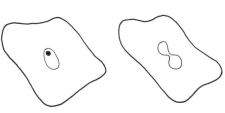

Animal cell at rest   Animal cell dividing

When a cell starts to divide, its .... changes to a dumbbell shape and its .... disappears altogether.

Frame A1.50

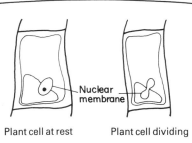

Plant cell at rest   Plant cell dividing

When a nucleus starts to divide, its .... or skin becomes stretched and its .... disappears.

Frame A1.51

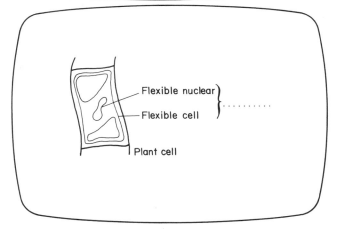

Flexible nuclear ⎫
                 ⎬ ....
Flexible cell   ⎭

Plant cell

Frame A1.52

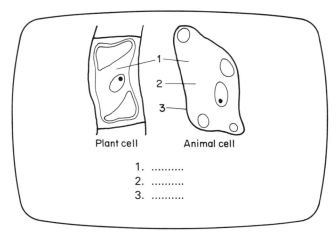

1. ....
2. ....
3. ....

Frame A1.53

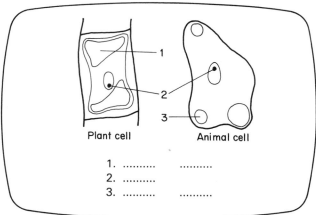

1. ....
2. ....
3. ....

Frame A1.54

One difference between plant cells and animal cells is that the former have .... cell walls made of .... and the latter have .... cell walls made of a thickish liquid called ectoplasm.

Frame A1.55

When a cell starts to divide its ....
stretches and the nucleus becomes dumbbell
shaped. Also, its .... disappears.

Frame A1.56

One important difference between animal and
plant cells is that in the latter surplus water
remains inside the cell in a permanent vacuole.

In an animal cell, however, its excess water in a
.... is expelled through a small hole in
the outer flexible skin, or .... of the cell.

Frame A1.57

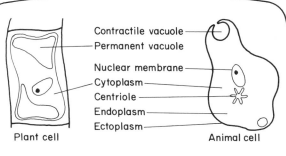

Contractile vacuole
Permanent vacuole
Nuclear membrane
Cytoplasm
Centriole
Endoplasm
Ectoplasm

Plant cell   Animal cell

In an animal cell there is a small star-shaped
body lying near the nucleus called a ....

Frame A1.58

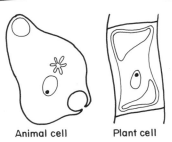

Animal cell   Plant cell

A plant cell doesn't have a .... near its nucleus.

Frame A1.59

Has an animal cell got a nucleus? ...
Has a plant cell got a nucleus? ...
Has an animal cell got a nucleolus when it is dividing? ...
Has a plant cell got a nucleolus when it is dividing? ...
Has an animal cell got a centriole? ...
Has a plant cell got a centriole? ...

(ANSWER Y OR N TO EACH ONE)

Frame A1.60

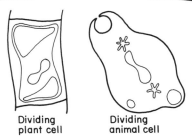

Dividing   Dividing
plant cell   animal cell

In a dividing plant cell its .... disappears and its nuclear membrane stretches. This happens in a dividing animal cell, too. In addition, its .... divides into two.

Frame A1.61

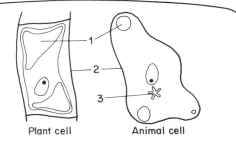

Plant cell   Animal cell

Explain in your own words what are three important differences between plant and animal cells.

Frame A1.62

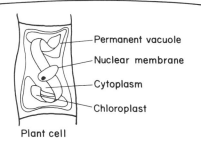

Permanent vacuole
Nuclear membrane
Cytoplasm
Chloroplast

Plant cell

Plants are green because they contain a chemical called chlorophyll. This green substance is found inside a ribbon-like body called a ....

Frame A1.63

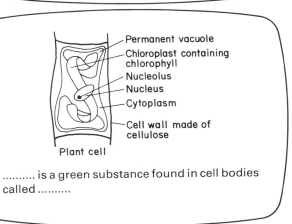

Permanent vacuole
Chloroplast containing chlorophyll
Nucleolus
Nucleus
Cytoplasm
Cell wall made of cellulose

Plant cell

.... is a green substance found in cell bodies called ....

Frame A1.64

Plant cell   Animal cell

Animals are not green because they contain no cell bodies called .... in their cells.

Frame A1.65

Animal cell   Plant cell

An animal cell has a .... which a plant cell has not got.
A plant cell has a .... which an animal cell has not got.

Frame A1.66

A plant nucleus contains a small round body called a .... and its cell usually contains a chloroplast made up from a substance called
....

Frame A1.67

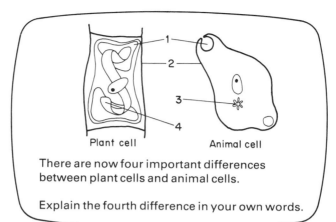

Plant cell   Animal cell

There are now four important differences
between plant cells and animal cells.

Explain the fourth difference in your own words.

Frame A1.68

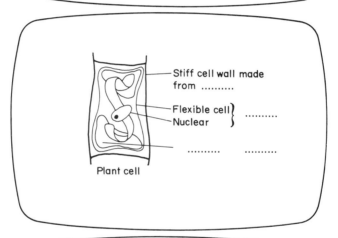

Stiff cell wall made
from ....

Flexible cell ⎫
Nuclear   ⎬ ....

....

Plant cell

Frame A1.69

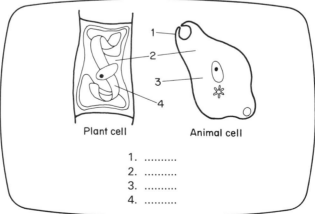

Plant cell   Animal cell

1. ....
2. ....
3. ....
4. ....

Frame A1.70

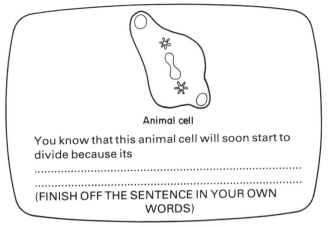

Animal cell

You know that this animal cell will soon start to divide because its

....

....

(FINISH OFF THE SENTENCE IN YOUR OWN WORDS)

Frame A1.71

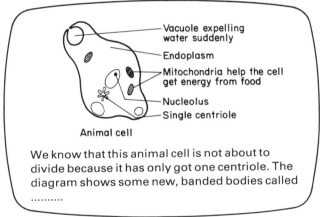

Vacuole expelling water suddenly

Endoplasm

Mitochondria help the cell get energy from food

Nucleolus

Single centriole

Animal cell

We know that this animal cell is not about to divide because it has only got one centriole. The diagram shows some new, banded bodies called

....

Frame A1.72

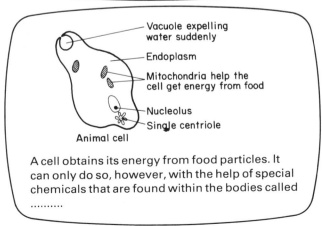

Vacuole expelling water suddenly

Endoplasm

Mitochondria help the cell get energy from food

Nucleolus

Single centriole

Animal cell

A cell obtains its energy from food particles. It can only do so, however, with the help of special chemicals that are found within the bodies called

....

Frame A1.73

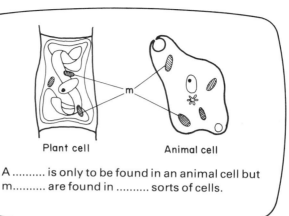

Plant cell   Animal cell

A .... is only to be found in an animal cell but
m .... are found in .... sorts of cells.

Frame A1.74

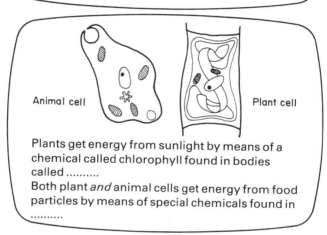

Animal cell   Plant cell

Plants get energy from sunlight by means of a
chemical called chlorophyll found in bodies
called ....
Both plant *and* animal cells get energy from food
particles by means of special chemicals found in
....

Frame A1.75

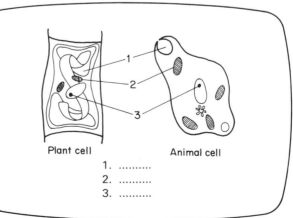

Plant cell   Animal cell

1. ....
2. ....
3. ....

Frame A1.76

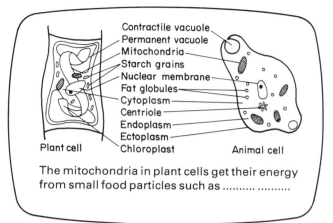

The mitochondria in plant cells get their energy from small food particles such as ....

Frame A1.77

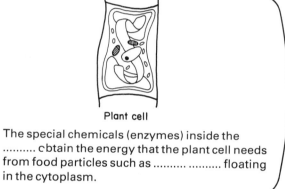

Plant cell

The special chemicals (enzymes) inside the .... obtain the energy that the plant cell needs from food particles such as .... floating in the cytoplasm.

Frame A1.78

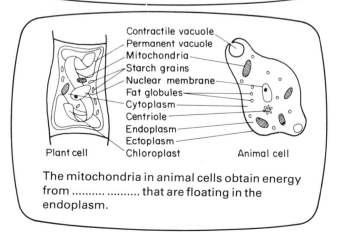

The mitochondria in animal cells obtain energy from .... that are floating in the endoplasm.

Frame A1.79

In a plant cell food is stored in the form of starch grains; in animal cells the food is in the form of ....

Frame A1.80

Food is stored in plant and animal cells in the form of small .... and .... respectively.

Frame A1.81

.... is a green chemical found in bodies called .... inside a plant cell.

Frame A1.82

Mitochondria are small bodies inside cells and have many small tunnels running through them containing chemicals called enzymes. These enzymes are able to release energy from ....
.... (in plant cells) and .... (in animal cells).

Frame A1.83

One major difference between plant cells and animal cells is that the former have .... walls made of a chemical called .... The ectoplasm of an animal cell, however, is ....

Frame A1.84

Draw a plant cell and label the following:

       Flexible cell membrane
       Cytoplasm
       Permanent vacuoles
       Nucleus
       Nucleolus
       Chloroplast
       Mitochondria
       Starch grains

Frame A1.85

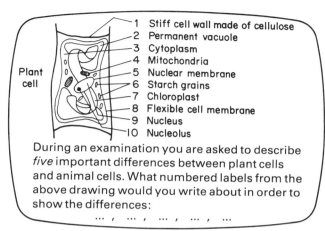

1 Stiff cell wall made of cellulose
2 Permanent vacuole
3 Cytoplasm
4 Mitochondria
5 Nuclear membrane
6 Starch grains
7 Chloroplast
8 Flexible cell membrane
9 Nucleus
10 Nucleolus

Plant cell

During an examination you are asked to describe *five* important differences between plant cells and animal cells. What numbered labels from the above drawing would you write about in order to show the differences:

... , ... , ... , ... , ...

Frame A1.86

Draw an animal cell and label the following:

Two centrioles
Nucleus (of the correct shape)
Flexible ectoplasm
Nuclear membrane
Endoplasm (at moment of expelling water)
Mitochondria
Fat globules

Frame A1.87

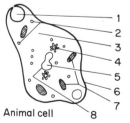

1
2
3
4
5
6
7
8

Animal cell

Which of these labels would you select and write about if you were asked to explain four important differences between the above cell and a plant cell?

... , ... , ... , ...

(the fifth difference: chloroplasts)

Frame A1.88

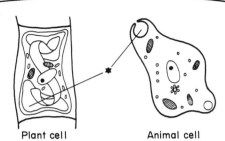

Plant cell   Animal cell

Write two or three sentences on one difference
between plant cells and animal cells as indicated
by the starred feature above.

Frame A1.89

Animal cell

When an animal cell starts to divide the ....
disappears.

Frame A1.90

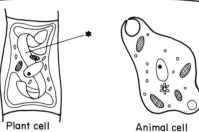

Plant cell   Animal cell

Write two or three sentences on one difference
between plant and animal cells as indicated by
the starred feature above.

Frame A1.91

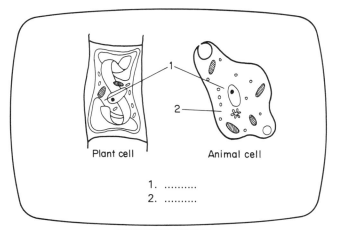

Plant cell   Animal cell

1. ....
2. ....

Frame A1.92

Are 'cytoplasm' and 'endoplasm' different terms
for the same thing in the animal cell?

(Y or N)

Frame A1.93

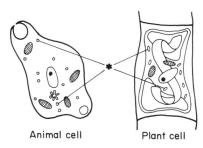

Animal cell   Plant cell

Write two or three sentences on one difference
between the two cells above by using the starred
features.

Frame A1.94

The chemicals called enzymes that help fat globules and starch grains to release their energy to the cell are to be found in tunnels inside small cell bodies called .... in animal and plant cells.

Frame A1.95

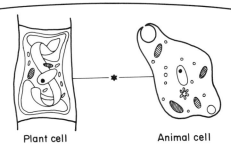

Plant cell   Animal cell

By reference to the starred items above, write two or three sentences on one major difference between the two cells.

Frame A1.96

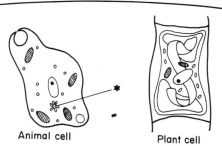

Animal cell   Plant cell

Write two sentences on one major difference between the two cells as prompted by the starred item above.

Frame A1.97

In plant and animal cells food is reserved in small bodies called .... and ....
respectively.

Frame A1.98

Draw and label a typical plant cell and an animal cell showing ten main features in each one.

Write a short passage describing five important differences between plant and animal cells.

Frame A1.99

Congratulations! You have now completed Unit 2 of this Biology course.

What you have learned in this Unit is now safely in your long-term memory. To prevent it fading, revise the question you have just answered:

    Tomorrow
    Then in a week's time
    Then in a month's time
    Then every two months until the
    examination

Appendix 2

Various CAL and CBT
authoring languages

IVL (Interactive Video Language) Dalroth Computer Products Ltd, 4 Half
   Moon Street, Mayfair, London W1V 7RA (01-493 2947).

WISE and SMART Wicat Systems Ltd, Edgbaston House, Duchess Place,
   Birmingham B16 8NH (021-454 7782).

TUTOR PLATO system, Control Data Ltd, 179/199 Shaftesbury Avenue,
   London WC2 8AR.

COMBAT Mills and Allen Communications Ltd, Broadwick House, 15/17
   Broadwick Street, London W1V 2AH.

MICROTEXT (for BBC 'B' Micro) Acorn Computers Ltd, Cambridge.

SuperPILOT (for Apple II) E. J. Arnold and Sons Ltd, Butterley Street, Leeds
   LS10 1AX.

CATS (Developed by J. R. Hartley) Software Training Department,
   Systime Computers Ltd, Millshaw Park, Leeds LS11 0LT.

IAS (Interactive Authoring System) McGraw-Hill Ltd, McGraw-Hill
   House, Maidenhead, Berkshire SL6 2QL (0628-23431).

The above is just a small sample of the many authoring systems that are
available.

Appendix 3

Centres of CAL activity

UNITED KINGDOM

BCS (British Computer Society), 13 Mansfield Street, London W1M 0BP.

CAMET (Centre for the Advancement of Mathematical Education in Technology), Loughborough University of Technology, Loughborough.

CATAM (University of Cambridge Computer Aided Teaching of Applied Mathematics), Department of Applied Mathematics and Theoretical Physics, Silver Street, Cambridge CB3 9EW.

CEDAR (Computers in Education as a Resource) Wild range of free publications. Imperial College Computer Centre, Exhibition Road, London SW7.

CEG (Computer Education Group) Publishes *Computer Education*. North Staffordshire Polytechnic Computer Centre, Blackheath Lane, Stafford.

CET (Council for Educational Technology) Publishes several publications including *CALNEWS*, 3 Devonshire Street, London W1N 2BA.

CHESS (Assocation of Computer Units in Colleges of Higher Education), Hatfield Polytechnic, Hatfield, Herts AL10 9AB.

EDINBURGH University, Department of Artificial Intelligence, Forest Hill, Edinburgh EH1 2QI. Probably the leading AI research group in the UK. Many publications in AI and CAL.

GAPE (Geographical Association Package Exchange), Department of Geography, University of Technology, Loughborough LE11 3TN.

ITMA (Investigation into Teaching with Microprocessor Assistance), College of St Mark and St John, Derriford Road, Plymouth, Devon PL6 8BH. Free newsletter.

LEEDS University, Computer Based Learning Unit, Leeds LS2 9JT. Under Dr J. R. Hartley, one of the leading CAL authorities in the country, this unit carries out a great deal of research. Several papers and publications are available.

MAPE (Micros and Primary Education), St Helen's School, Bluntisham, Cambridgeshire. Is associated with *Microscope* published by John Lane, Newman College, Bartley Green, Birmingham B32 3NT.

MEP (Microelectronics Education Programme), Cheviot House, Coach Lane Campus, Newcastle upon Tyne NE7 7XA. Has 14 regional centres and full-time organizers providing services to schools and CAL writers.

MICE (Microcomputers in Computer Education), Room 231C, The County Hall, London SE1.

MUSE (Microcomputer Users in School Education), Freepost, Bromsgrove, Worcestershire, B61 7BR. Has a library of CAL programs and publishes a journal, *Computers in Schools.*

NCC (National Computing Centre), Oxford Road, Manchester M1 7ED. One of the main UK advisory centres for microcomputing in business and educational applications. Also publishes books and research reports.

NPLC (Network of Programmed Learning Centres), The Polytechnic, Holly Bank Road, Huddersfield HD3 3BP.

OPEN UNIVERSITY, Institute of Educational Technology, Walton Hall, Milton Keynes, Bucks, MK7 6AA. The Director, Professor David Hawkridge, is possibly the UK's leading figure in the whole field of educational technology. A free CAL bibliography is available together with details of many other projects and research.

OPEN UNIVERSITY, Committee on Communication Technology, Walton Hall, Milton Keynes, Bucks, MK7 6AA.

PEAT Marwick, Mitchell and Co, 5th floor, 1 Puddle Dock, Blackfriars, London EC4 3PD. Consultants J. Fielden and P. K. Pearson have produced several case studies on the costs of educational innovation.

QUEEN MARY College (University of London), Faculty of Engineering, Mile End Road, London E1 4NS. Has originated an engineering science CAL program exchange service.

RESEARCH MACHINES Ltd, Mill Street, Oxford OX2 0BW. A microcomputer manufacturer which is getting directly involved in the production of good CAL software.

SAGSET (Society for Academic Gaming and Simulations in Education and Training), Centre for Extension Studies, University of Technology, Loughborough, Leics LE11 3TU. Membership open to anyone interested in developing computerized simulations and games for learning objectives.

SINCLAIR RESEARCH Stanhope Road, Camberley, Surrey. Another microcomputer manufacturer directly involved with CAL

UNITED STATES

There are so many academic, commercial and voluntary centres of CAL activity in the United States that only a small selection can be included here.

ACADEMY for Educational Development Inc, 680 Fifth Avenue, New York, NY 10019. CAL co-ordination. Non-profitmaking.

AGENCY for Instructional Television, Box A, Bloomington, IN 47402. Non-profitmaking American–Canadian organization. Makes many television materials available in other formats.

AMERICAN Education Research Association (AERA), 1230 17th Street NW, Washington, DC 20036. International organization of research and applications in 60 special interest groups. Publishes monthly magazines.

AMERICAN Institutes for Research in the Behavioural Sciences, Box 1113, Palo Alto, CA 94302. Research and publications.

AMERICAN Society for Information Science, 1010 16th Street NW, Washington, DC 20036.

AMERICAN Society for Training and Development, Suite 305, 600 Maryland Avenue, SW, Washington, DC 20024. Non-profitmaking association supplying programs and services to over 21 000 members.

ASSOCIATION for Computer-Based Instructional Systems, Box 70189, Los Angeles, CA 90070. Exchange of information. Various publications.

ASSOCIATION for Educational Communications and Technology (AECT), 1126 Sixteenth Street, NW, Washington, DC 20036. A professional association available to CAL writers. Many publications.

BASIC Education Computers Inc, 2772 S Randolph Street, Arlington, VA 22206.

BORG-WARNER Educational Systems, 600 W University Drive, Arlington Heights, IL 60004.

CHILDREN'S Television Workshop, 1 Lincoln Plaza, New York, NY 10023. Research materials; numerous periodicals.

COASTLINE Community College, 10231 Slater Avenue, Fountain Valley, CA 92708. Huge variety of distance-learning courses.

CONDUIT 100 Lindquist Center, The University of Iowa, PO Box 388, Iowa City, IA. Non-profitmaking agency delivering proven CAL programs in 13 different disciplines. Publishes *The CONDUIT Author's Guide* and many more books and magazines.

CURRICULUM Materials Clearinghouse, University Microfilms, 300 North Zeeb Road, Ann Arbor, MI 48106. Information Exchange in association with ERIC clearing-house.

EDUCATIONAL Facilities Laboratories, 850 Third Avenue, New York City, NY 10022. Research supported by Ford Foundation; many different publications.

EDUCATIONAL Development Laboratories, Division of McGraw-Hill Inc, 1221 Avenue of the Americas, New York, NY 10020.

EDUCATIONAL Products Information Exchange, EPIE Institute, 475 Riverside Drive, New York, NY. No commercial ties and is school-based. Has independent Testing Laboratory. Many publications.

GOULD Inc, Educational Systems Division, 4423 Arden Drive, El Monte, CA 91731.

HENDERSHOT Bibliography, 4114 Ridgewood, Bay City, MI 48706. Probably the best source book on CAL.

ILLINOIS University, Computer-Based Research Laboratory, 252 Engineering Research Laboratory, Urbana, IL 61801. Research and development of CERL version of PLATO. Many publications. Consults with CAL writers.

INTERNATIONAL Congress for Individualised Instruction, ICII, Biology Department, Fordham University, Bronx, NY 10458. Publishes newsletter *One-to-One* with evaluations of different forms of CAL.

INTERNATIONAL Council for Computers in Education, Department of Computer and Information Science, University of Oregon, Eugene, OR 97403. 6000 individual members.

LEARNING Systems Inc, 1535 Fen Park Drive, Fenton, MO 63026.

MICROCOMPUTER Research Center (MRC), Box 18, Teachers College, Columbia University, New York, NY 10027. Provides consultation and information on educational uses of microcomputers. Software evaluation.

MINNESOTA Educational Computing Consortium, 2520 Broadway Drive, St Paul, MN 55113. One of the largest and most highly respected organizations in the United States using computers in education. Have developed a large range of fully tested material for use on mainframe terminals or microcomputers.

NATIONAL Center for Research in Vocational Education, Ohio State University, 1960 Kenny Road, Columbus, OH 43210. Non-profitmaking with international membership. Deals with 45000 requests a year for information. Several monthly newsletters and magazines.

NATIONAL SOCIETY for Performance and Instruction (NSPI) (formerly National Society for Programmed Instruction), 1126 Sixteenth Street NW, Washington, DC 20036. 2000 members and publishes *Performance and Instruction Journal*.

NATIONAL Video Clearinghouse Inc, PO Box 3, Syosset, New York 11791. For the video-disc CAL writer. Several magazines.

NEW YORK State University, Faculty of Educational Studies, New Media Lab and Programmed Instruction Center, 210 Baldy Hall, Anherst, NY 14260. List of publications available on request.

THE NETWORK Inc, 290 South Main Street, Andover, MA 01810. Non-profitmaking educational service. Publication list available.

NICEM (National Information Center for Educational Media), University of Southern California, University Park, Los Angeles, CA 90007. 500000 entries of non-print media in current data base. Each entry contains brief synopsis.

PUBLIC Service Satellite Consortium, Suite 907, 1660 L Street, NW, Washington, DC 20036. Non-profitmaking international clearing-house organization. Has profitmaking subsidiary, SATSERV, for satellite transmission.

SIMULATION and Gaming Association (SAGA), 4833 Greentree Road, Lebanon, OH 45036.

SAN FRANCISCO State University, Audiovisual and Instructional Television Center, 1600 Holloway Avenue, San Francisco, CA 94132. Has developed a 35 channel cable system for over 60000 homes including CAL services.

SINGER EDUCATION Systems, 3750 Monroe Avenue, Rochester, NY 14603.

SONY Learning Systems, Educational Electronics Corp, 213 N Cedar Avenue, Inglewood, CA 90301.

TUTORSYSTEMS, Division of Sargent-Welch Scientific Co, 7300 N Linder Avenue, Skokie, Il 60076.

NB As in the UK, all major US book publishers have recently instituted CAL departments and are interested in CAL software.

JAPAN

AICHI University of Education, Centre for Educational Technology, 1 Hirosawa, Igawa-cho, Kariya City, Aichi Prefecture, 448.

AKITA University, Centre for Educational Technology, Faculty of Education, 1-1 Tegatagakuencho, Akita City, 010.

FUKUI University, Research and Guidance Centre of Teaching Practice, Faculty of Education, 9-1, 3-chome, Bunkyo, Fukui-shi.

FUKUOKA University of Education, Centre for Educational Technology, 279 Akama, Munakata-machi, Munakata-gun, Fukuoka Prefecture, 811-41.

HOKKAIDO University of Education, Centre for Educational Technology, Nishi 13 Minami 22, Cho-ku, Sapporo City, Hokkaido, 064.

JAPAN Audio-Visual Educational Association, 1-17-1 Toranomon, Minato-ku, Tokyo, 105. Non-profitmaking organization aimed at promoting CAL and other audio-visual aids. Has an international information centre. Publishes handbooks and catalogues; and organizes the main Japanese educational exhibition every year.

JAPAN Council of Educational Technology Centres, c/o Unesco and International Affairs Bureau, Ministry of Education, Science and Culture, Kasumigaseki, Tokyo, 100.

KAGAWA University, Centre for Educational Technology, Faculty of

Education, 1-1 Saiwa-cho, Takamatsui City, Kagawa Prefecture 760. Recently built in the new 'science city' of Japan, Kagawa University carries out a substantial range of research into CAL and other microcomputer applications. Publishes *KACET News*.

KAMZAWA University, Educational Technology Centre, Faculty of Education, 1-1 Maranouchi, Kanazawa City, 920. Specializes in childrens' programs.

KYOTO University of Education, Centre for Educational Research and TRaining, 1 Fujinomori, Fukakusa, Fushimi-ku, Kyoto City, 612. Considerable CAL research. Publishes software called *APPER* (Analysing Program Packages for Educational Research) and *Technical Reports*.

LL SCHOOL (Osaka School), 2F Osaka-Ekimae-Daiichi Building, 4-20 Sonazaki-ue, Kita-ku, Osaka, 530.

MATSUSHITA Audio-Visual Educational Foundation, Shuwa-Onarimon Building, 6-1-1 Shinbashi, Minato-ku, Tokyo, 105. Plans and coordinates much CAL research in Japan. Evaluates software.

NAGASAKI University, Centre for Educational Technology, Faculty of Education, 1-14 Bunkyo-cho, Nagasaki City, 852. Specializes in distance-learning for five remote islands (the NIGHT project). Publications include *Teaching Material* and annual *Studies in Teaching-Learning Programs*.

SHINSHU University, Educational Technology Centre, Faculty of Education, 6 Nishinagano-machi, Nagano City, 380.

TOKYO Institute of Technology, Centre for Research and Development of Educational Technology (CRADLE), 2-12-1 Oh-akayama, Meguro-ku, Tokyo, 152. An advanced research centre in video material, optical fibre teaching systems and specialized microcomputers.

References

1. Gershuny, J. (1978) *After Industrial Society: The Emerging Self-Service Economy*, Macmillan, London.
2. Martin, J. (1981) *Telematic Society*, Prentice-Hall, Englewood Cliffs, New Jersey.
3. Stonier, T. (1983) *The Wealth of Information*, Thames Methuen, London.
4. Papert, S. (1980) *Mindstorms: Children, Computers and Powerful Ideas*, Harvester Press, London.
5. Donaldson, M. (1978) *Children's Minds*, Fontana/Collins, Glasgow.
6. Skinner, B. F. (1954) The science of learning and the art of teaching. *Harvard Educational Review*, **24**.
7. Skinner, B. F. (1965) *Walden Two*, Macmillan, London.
8. Chomsky, N. (1959) A review of B. F. Skinner's 'Verbal Behaviour'. *Language*, **35**.
9. Chomsky, N. (1968) *Language and Mind*, Harcourt, Brace and World, New York.
10. Skinner, B. F. (1972) *Beyond Freedom and Dignity*, Jonathan Cape, London.
11. Young, J. Z. (1978) *Programs of the Brain*, Oxford University Press, Oxford.
12. Sharpe, R. (1983) Research to find the big hit. *Computing*, 23 June, p. 24.
13. Hartley, J. R. (1978) *Computer Assisted Learning*, Computer Based Learning Unit, Leeds University.
14. Blakemore, C. (1977) *Mechanics of the Mind*, Cambridge University Press, Cambridge.
15. Piaget, J. (1970) *Science of Education and the Psychology of the Child*, Orion, New York.
16. Jaynes, J. (1982) *The Origin of Consciousness in the Breakdown of the Bicameral Mind*, Penguin, London.
17. Watson, J. D. (1970) *The Double Helix*, Penguin, London.
18. Bloom, B.S., Engelhart, M.D., Furst, E.J. *et al* (1975) *Taxonomy of Educational Objectives (Handbooks I, II and III)*, David McKay, New York.
19. Gagné, R. M. (1977) *The Conditions of Learning*, Holt, Rinehart and Winston, New York.
20. Lashley, K. S. (1950) In search of the engram. *Symp. Exp. Biol.*, **4**, 454.
21. *Writers' & Artists' Yearbook*, Adam and Charles Black, London.
22. *Courseware Market Report*, Shotwell and Associates, San Francisco, California (1981).
23. *Educational Software: the Next Boost to the Microcomputer Market*, IPI, Copenhagen (1983).

Recommended bibliography

CAL SECTION

Atkinson, R. V. and Wilson, H. A. (1969) *Computer-Assisted Instruction: a Book of Readings*, Academic Press, New York.

Bailey, D. E. (ed.) (1978) *Computer Science in Social and Behavioural Science Education*, Educational Technology Publications, Englewood Cliffs, New Jersey.

Baker, F. B. (1978) *Computer Managed Instruction Theory and Practice*, Educational Technology Publications, Englewood Cliffs, New Jersey.

Beech, G. (ed.) (1979) *Computer Assisted Learning in Science Education*, Pergamon Press, Oxford.

Black, J. (1969) *Computer for Education: Council for Educational Technology Working Paper No 1*, Councils and Education Press, London.

Bork, A. (1981) *Learning with Computers*, Digital Press, Bedford, Mass.

Brown, J. S. and Sleeman, D. (1982) *Intelligent Tutoring Systems*, Academic Press, New York.

Burke, R. L. (1982) *CAI Sourcebook*, Prentice-Hall, Englewood Cliffs, New Jersey.

Dean, C. and Whitlock, Q. (1983) *A Handbook of Computer Based Training*, Kogan Page, London.

Fiddy, P. and Wharry, D. (1983) *Micros in Early Education*, Longman, London.

Hartley, J. (1978) *Designing Instructional Tests*, Kogan Page, London.

Hartley, J. (1978) *Computer Assisted Learning: A Review of Research and Applications*, Computer Based Learning Unit, University of Leeds.

Hickey, A. E. (1974) *Research Guidelines for Computer-Assisted Instruction*, Albert E. Hickey Associates, Newburyport, Mass.

Hills, P. (1981) *The Future of the Printed Word*, Open University Press, Milton Keynes.

Hooper, R. (1977) *The National Development Programme in Computer-Assisted Learning*, Council for Educational Technology, London.

Howe, J. A. M. and Ross, P. M. (1981) *Microcomputers in Secondary Education*, Kogan Page, London.

Hoye, R. E. and Wang, A. C. (eds.) (1975) *Index to Computer Based Learning*, Educational Technology Publications, Englewood Cliffs, New Jersey.

Hsido, T. C. (ed.) (1977) *World Encyclopaedia of Computer Education and Research*, Science and Technology Press, Washington DC.

Huntingdon, J. F. (1979) *Computer-Assisted Instruction Using BASIC*, Educational Technology Publications, Englewood Cliffs, New Jersey.

Jones, R. (1980) *Microcomputers: Their Uses in Primary Schools*, Council for Educational Technology, London.

Maddison, A. (1982) *Microcomputers in the Classroom*, Hodder and Stoughton, London.

Maddison, J. (1983) *Education in the Microelectronics Era*, Open University Press, Milton Keynes.

Kemmis, S., Atkin, R. and Wright, E. (1979) *How Do Students Learn: Evaluation of NDPCAL, (National Development Programme in Computer Assisted Learning)*, University of East Anglia, Norwich.

Nelson, T. (1977) *The Home Computer Revolution*, Distributors, South Bend, Indiana.

Osborne, C. W. (ed.) *International Yearbook of Educational and Instructional Technology*, Association for Educational and Training Technology/Kogan Page/Nichols, London.

Papert, S. (1980) *Mindstorms*, Harvester Press, London.

Roberts, N., Andersen, D. R., Deal, R.N. *et al.* (1983) *Introduction to Computer Simulation*, Addison-Wesley, London.

Rushby, N. (ed.) (1981) *Selected Readings in Computer Based Learning*, Kogan Page, London.

Rushby, N. (1979) *Introduction to Educational Computing*, Croom Helm, London.

Seidel, R. J. and Rubin, M. (eds.) (1977) *Computers and Communications: Implications for Education*, Academic Press, New York.

Shepherd, I. D. H., Cooper, Z. A. and Walke, D. R. F. (1980) *Computer Assisted Learning in Geography*, Council for Educational Technology, London.

Sledge, D. (ed.) (1979) *Microcomputers in Education*, Council for Educational Technology, London.

Sleeman, D. and Brown, J. R. (1980) *Intelligent Computer Tutors*, Academic Press, New York.

BRAIN SYSTEMS SECTION

Introductory

Argyle, M. (1975) *Bodily Communication*, Methuen, London.

Barash, D. (1980) *Sociobiology: The Whisperings Within*, Fontana/Collins, London.

Blakemore, C. (1977) *Mechanics of the Mind*, Cambridge University Press, London.

Calder, N. (1970) *The Mind of Man*, BBC, London.

Campbell, H. J. (1973) *The Pleasure Areas*, Eyre Methuen, London.

Dawkins, R. (1976) *The Selfish Gene*, Oxford University Press, Oxford.

Donaldson, M. (1978) *Children's Minds*, Fontana/Collins, Glasgow.

Farb, P. (1978) *Humankind*, Triad Paladin, St Albans.

Hinde, R. A. (1982) *Ethology*, Fontana, London.

Hubel, D. H. (1979) The Brain. *Scientific American*, **214**, 44.

Leakey, R. E. and Lewin, R. (1978) *Origins*, Macdonald and Jane's, London.

Luria, A. R. (1976) *The Working Brain*, Penguin, London.

Midgley, M. (1979) *Beast and Man: The Roots of Human Nature*, Methuen, London.

Ornstein, R. E. (1975) *The Psychology of Consciousness*, Penguin, London.

Penfield, W. (1975) *The Mystery of the Mind*, Princeton University Press, Princeton, New Jersey.

Rose, S. (1976) *The Conscious Brain*, Penguin, London.

Thompson, R. (1975) *Introduction to Physiological Psychology*, Harber International, New York.

Walter, W. B. (1968) *The Living Brain*, Penguin, London.

More advanced

Boddy, J. (1978) *Brain Systems and Psychological Concepts*, John Wiley, Chichester.

Eccles, J. C. (1973) *The Understanding of the Brain*, McGraw-Hill, New York.

Jaynes, J. (1982) *The Origin of Consciousness in the Breakdown of the Bicameral Mind*, Penguin, London.

Lumsden, C. J. and Wilson, E. O. (1981) *Genes, Mind and Culture: The Coevolutionary Process*, Harvard University Press, Cambridge, Mass.

Olds, J. (1977) *Drives and Reinforcements*, Raven Press, New York.

Penfield, W. (1967) *The Excitable Cortex in Conscious Man*, Liverpool University Press, Liverpool.

Popper, K. R. and Eccles, J. C. (1972) *The Self and Its Brain*, Springer-Verlag, Berlin.

Rolls, E. T. (1975) *The Brain and Reward*, Pergamon Press, Oxford.

Wilson, E. O. (1975) *Sociobiology, The New Synthesis*, Harvard University Press, Cambridge, Mass.

Wooldridge, D. E. (1963) *The Machinery of the Brain*, McGraw-Hill, New York.

Young, J. Z. (1978) *Programs of the Brain*, Oxford University Press, Oxford.

TOMORROW'S WORLD SECTION

Bell, D. (1976) *The Coming of Post-Industrial Society*, Penguin, London.

Evans, C. (1979) *The Mighty Micro*, Coronet/Hodder and Stoughton, London.

Gershuny, J. (1978) *After Industrial Society: The Emerging Self-Service Economy*, Macmillan, London.

Kahn, H. (ed.) (1974) *The Future of the Corporation*, Mason and Lipscomb, New York.

Laurie, P. (1980) *The Micro Revolution*, Futura, London.

Martin, J. (1981) *Telematic Society: A Challenge for Tomorrow*, Prentice-Hall, Englewood Cliffs, New Jersey.

Naisbitt, J. (1983) *Megatrends: Ten New Directions Transforming Our Lives*, Warner Books, New York.

Osborn, A. (1979) *Running Wild: The Next Industrial Revolution*, Osborn/McGraw-Hill, Berkeley, California.

Pawley, M. (1975) *The Private Future*, Pan, London.

Stephenson, H. (1972) *The Coming Clash: The Impact of Multinational Corporations on National States*, Saturday Review Press, New York.

Stonier, T. (1983) *The Wealth of Information*, Thames Methuen, London.

Index